SOUTHEASTERN COMMUNITY COLLEGE
Southeastern Community
College Library
Whiteville, NC 28472

NORTH CAROLINA
STATE BOARD OF EDUCATION
DEPT. OF COMMUNITY COLLEGES
LIBRARIES

D1776950

THE
NATURE LOVER'S
KNAPSACK

THE Nature Lover's Knapsack

AN ANTHOLOGY OF POEMS FOR LOVERS OF THE OPEN ROAD

Edited by
Edwin Osgood Grover

Enlarged Edition

Granger Poetry Library

GRANGER BOOK CO., INC.
Great Neck, NY

First Published 1927
Enlarged Edition 1947
Reprinted 1979

INTERNATIONAL STANDARD BOOK NUMBER
0-89609-114-7

LIBRARY OF CONGRESS CATALOG NUMBER
78-73488

PRINTED IN THE UNITED STATES OF AMERICA

To

M. L. G.

Who has shared with me
the
Joys of "Knapsack Carrying"
along Life's road

On Knapsack Carrying

WE are all knapsack carriers. And none of us travels far on the road of Life without discovering certain things which we would not be without,—things that seem indispensable to our happiness. These indispensable things we put, often unconsciously, into our knapsack to carry with us during the remainder of the journey.

The kinds of things we "tote" in our knapsack vary with the different stages of our journey. We begin by collecting pebbles for our sling shot, and in lieu of a literal knapsack we hide them in our boy's pocket. A little farther along the journey we discover that marbles, or stamps, or arrowheads are the things that are indispensable to our happiness, and we gradually shift our knapsack load to meet the newer need.

Still later in life some of us accumulate coins and bank notes, stocks and mortgages, and other passing trifles that for the moment seem the only indispensable things to our happiness. We work ourselves sick, we sacrifice our friends, we succeed so well that soon our knapsack is too full for us to carry, and we go to some friendly banker and ask him to put it in his safety deposit vault where we may worry about it to our hearts' content. And there it rests until we come to die, and the only joy it has brought us is the cheap joy of accumulation.

Some of us, however, by force of circumstance or by deliberate choice, begin early in life to collect in our knapsacks beautiful memories of sunsets, of cloud-capped hills and wind-swept plains, of deep-flowing rivers and talking brooks, memories of the infinite sky and the eternal sea, of bird songs and blossoms, of trembling trees and all the lovely things of nature. And after the first ecstasy of discovery, these things gradually become the indispensable things of our happiness and of our lives. Every spring these joys are reborn in us, and every autumn they flare up with the first reddening tree. Each month in the cycle of the year holds its unforgettable thrill, its reminder of ancient glories and happy memories.

Next to the recollection of beauties we have seen with our own eyes and carried long in the knapsack of our memory, there is no joy greater than walking afield with the poets, and spending an afternoon discovering new beauties and new meanings in Nature.

Soon or late every nature lover makes a collection of those poems that remind him of his own memories. These he treasures in his knapsack, and as the seasons come and go he takes them out to feed his soul and to refresh his spirit as he travels hopefully along the road of Life.

I would not for the world deprive any one of this pleasure. I only hope that this knapsack of nature poetry will be found a worthy travelling companion for every nature lover. It cannot be exhaustive, and it is in no sense a reference book. Its only purpose is to serve as a friendly guide to many of the most beautiful nature poems by English and American authors. They lead one over an unknown trail with here a glimpse of sea, there a racing cloud, now the patter of April rain, and the smell of apple blossoms. Open the book where you will, and it leads you off through field or forest, by babbling brook or singing sea.

An anthology necessarily implies an individual choice, and the selections within have been chosen almost without exception for the pleasure they have given me. Because I believe that Lyric poetry is the highest form of poetic expression, I have given the preference to poems that possess this singing quality.

In spite of the fact that in much of the poetry of the last twenty-five years the lyric note has been sadly absent, yet the book contains many exquisite lyrics by the "younger generation" which shows the persistence of this timeless quality of all great poetry.

I wish to acknowledge frankly my indebtedness to many who have preceded me in the making of anthologies; and to scores of authors and their publishers who have so generously given permission for me to include their poems. It is a goodly fellowship. If, after all, I have left out your favorite nature poem, please tell me so.

EDWIN OSGOOD GROVER

Preface to the Enlarged Edition

A word of appreciation seems appropriate in commemoration of this enlarged edition of *The Nature Lover's Knapsack*.

It now appears packed with thirty-seven additional pages of carefully chosen nature poems representing many of the new, as well as older poets, who have been inspired to write distinguished verse revealing the intimate bond existing between what we call nature and human nature. The mystic tie lies far deeper than many of us realize. We are all part of one another, and no life of whatever kind liveth unto itself.

The compiler again expresses his appreciation to the authors and publishers who have made this enlarged edition possible. May *The Nature Lover's Knapsack* continue to carry its happy burden of pleasure to everyone who, like the Ancient Mariner—

> "loveth best
> All things both great and small;
> For the dear Lord, who loveth us,
> He made and loveth all."

—E. O. G.

What the Knapsack Holds

The Lure of the Road

In Spring-Time	*W. H. Davies*	1
I Must Out and Play Again	*Kathleen Millay*	2
A Wanderer's Song	*John Masefield*	3
The Singer's Quest	*Odell Shepherd*	3
Toil of the Trail	*Hamlin Garland*	4
Two Old Men	*Louise Driscoll*	5
The Best Road of All	*Charles Hanson Towne*	6
The Cry of the Dreamer	*John Boyle O'Reilly*	7
Highways	*Leslie Nelson Jennings*	8
Afoot and Light-hearted	*Walt Whitman*	9
The Path that Leads to Nowhere	*Corinne Roosevelt Robinson*	9
City-Weary	*Edgar A. Guest*	10
The Faun	*Richard Hovey*	12
The Call of the Wild	*Robert W. Service*	13
A City Voice	*Theodosia Garrison*	15
Fishing	*Edgar A. Guest*	16
Camping Song	*Bliss Carman*	17
The Green Inn	*Theodosia Garrison*	18
Wanderlust	*Isabel Ecclestine Mackay*	19
Song	*Georgiana Goddard King*	19
In City Streets	*Ada Smith*	20
Up! Up! My Friend, and Quit Your Books	*William Wordsworth*	21
Road Song	*James Stewart Montgomery*	22
Walking at Night	*Amory Hare*	23
Road Song	*W. G. Tinckom-Fernandez*	24
A Song of the Open Road	*Louis J. McQuilland*	25
A Maine Trail	*Gertrude H. McGiffert*	27
The Spell of the Pool	*L. Burton Crane, Jr.*	28
The Lake	*Eleanour Norton*	29
The Great Outdoors	*Maud Russell*	29
Come, Spur Away	*Thomas Randolph*	30
Hunting Song	*Richard Hovey*	31
The Call	*Cora D. Fenton*	31
The King's Highway	*John Steven McGroarty*	32
God Made this Day for Me	*Edgar A. Guest*	34
The Country Faith	*Norman Gale*	35
Yellow Warblers	*Katharine Lee Bates*	35
Reveille	*Louis Untermeyer*	36

Growing Things

The Mangroves Dance	*Rose Strong Hubbell*	37
Who Plants a Dogwood Tree	*Mabel Brown*	38
Afoot	*Charles G. D. Roberts*	39
Grace for Gardens	*Louise Driscoll*	40
My Garden	*Thomas E. Brown*	41
April	*John Vance Cheney*	41
A Song the Grass Sings	*Charles G. Blanden*	42
The Young Dandelion	*Dinah Mulock Craik*	42
Sunflowers	*Clinton Scollard*	43
Wishing	*William Allingham*	44
Rain	*Lucy Larcom*	44
To the Dandelion	*James Russell Lowell*	45
The Grass	*Walt Whitman*	47
Buttercups	*Wilfrid C. Thorley*	47
The Lilac	*Humbert Wolfe*	48
The Hollyhocks	*Ray Laurance*	48
The Ragged Regiment	*Alice Williams Brotherton*	49
Marigolds	*Bliss Carman*	49
In a Garden	*Theda Kenyon*	50
The Dandelions	*Helen Gray Cone*	51
Rhodora	*Ralph Waldo Emerson*	52
Daisies	*Bliss Carman*	53
Out in the Fields with God	*Louise Imogen Guiney*	53
The Blackbird	*Humbert Wolfe*	54
The Robin	*Emily Dickinson*	54
Clover	*John B. Tabb*	55
A Conversation	*Sara Hamilton Birchall*	55
A Yellow Pansy	*Helen Gray Cone*	56
The Answer	*Sara Hamilton Birchall*	57
A Prayer	*Edwin Markham*	57

The Kinship of the Trees

Girl in a Tree	*Frances Frost*	59
Year In, Year Out	*Kathleen Millay*	60
Twilight of the Wood	*Léonie Adams*	60
Tree Feelings	*Charlotte Perkins Gilman*	61
A B C's in Green	*Leonora Speyer*	62
O Dreamy, Gloomy, Friendly Trees	*Herbert Trench*	62
God, When You Thought of a Pine Tree	*Unknown*	63

The House of the Trees	*Ethelwyn Wetherald*	64
Trees	*Bliss Carman*	65
The Trees and the Master	*Sidney Lanier*	66
The Trees	*Samuel Valentine Cole*	67
Three Trees	*Christopher Morley*	68
What Do We Plant?	*Henry Abbey*	69
Trees	*Henry van Dyke*	70
The Trees	*Lucy Larcom*	71
Good Company	*Karl Wilson Baker*	71
The Green Tree in the Fall	*Jessie B. Rittenhouse*	72

The Call of the Sea

Bag-Pipes at Sea	*Clinton Scollard*	73
Young Sea	*Carl Sandburg*	74
Sea-Fever	*John Masefield*	75
A Son of the Sea	*Bliss Carman*	75
Dreams of the Sea	*William H. Davies*	76
Going Down in Ships	*Harry Kemp*	77
The Waves of Breffny	*Eva Gore-Booth*	78
Short Beach	*Richard Hovey*	79
Sea Call	*Margaret Widdemer*	79
Ship-Love	*Ethel E. Mannin*	80
The Sea	*Nora Hopper*	81
Coquette	*Keith Stuart*	82
The Deep-Water Man	*James Stuart Montgomery*	82
Sea Longing	*Harold Vinal*	84
Had I the Choice	*Walt Whitman*	84
Gray	*Oscar Williams*	85
A Pagan Hymn	*John Runcie*	85
As the Tide Comes In	*Cale Young Rice*	86
A Wet Sheet and a Flowing Sea	*Allan Cunningham*	87
The Undersong	*Fiona Macleod*	88
Gray Rocks and Grayer Sea	*Charles G. D. Roberts*	89
The Sea	*Bryan Waller Procter*	89
The Sea Road	*Martha Haskell Clark*	91
The Sea	*Richard Hovey*	92
The World Is Too Much with Us	*William Wordsworth*	94
Sunrise	*Robert Browning*	94
Song of the Sea	*Richard Burton*	95
Farewell	*Katherine Tynan*	96
The Return	*Algernon Charles Swinburne*	97

The Port o' Hearts Desire	*John Steven McGroarty*	99
Sea-Urge	*Unknown*	100
The Ocean .	*Lord Byron*	100
A Song of Desire	*Frederic Lawrence Knowles*	102
A Sea Change	*Dorothy Peace*	103
Twilight at Sea	*Amelia C. Welby*	103
Sea-Song	*Martha Haskell Clark*	104
Deep Down	*James Stuart Montgomery*	104
Flood Tide	*Marjorie Alice Miller*	105

The Winds of Heaven

South Wind	*Siegfried Sassoon*	107
The Roaring Frost	*Alice Meynell*	107
Cook County	*Archibald MacLeish*	108
Do You Fear the Wind?	*Hamlin Garland*	109
Hark to the Shouting Wind	*Henry Timod*	109
Who Hath Seen the Wind	*Christina Rossetti*	110
Wind	*John Galsworthy*	110
The Sea-Wind	*Arthur Ketchum*	111
I Meant to Do My Work Today	*Richard Le Gallienne*	111
That Wind is Best	*Caroline Atherton Mason*	112
Happy Wind	*William H. Davies*	112
Wind-Litany	*Margaret Widdemer*	113
A Morning	*Theodosia Garrison*	114
The Wind's Life	*Harry Kemp*	115
The Mystic	*Cale Young Rice*	115

The Hillborn

Climb	*Winifred Welles*	117
The Mountain Sat	*Emily Dickinson*	118
One Kind of Humility	*Jean Starr Untermeyer*	118
The Cry of the Hillborn	*Bliss Carman*	119
Up a Hill and a Hill	*Fannie Stearns Davis*	120
Hills	*Arthur Guiterman*	121
Again Among the Hills	*Richard Hovey*	122
Hill Hunger	*Joseph Auslander*	124
Afternoon on a Hill	*Edna St. Vincent Millay*	125
The Hills	*Theodosia Garrison*	125
On a Hill	*Irene Rutherford McLeod*	126
The Most-Sacred Mountain	*Eunice Tietjens*	127

Traveler's Joy

Sea-Chill	*Arthur Guiterman*	129
Bring Me the Sunset in a Cup	*Emily Dickinson*	130
Traveller's Joy	*Arthur Ketchum*	131
Ellis Park	*Helen Hoyt*	132
Afoot	*C. Fox-Smith*	133
The Going of His Feet	*Harry Kemp*	134
Down East and Up Along	*Edwin Osgood Grover*	135
Joys of the Road	*Bliss Carman*	136
Song of the Open	*Sara Hamilton Birchall*	139
Rebellion	*Stephen Chalmers*	140
The Tree-Top Road	*May Riley Smith*	142
Early Morning at Bargis	*Hermann Hagedorn*	143
Denial	*Lancaster Pollard*	144
"A La Belle Étoile"	*Sara Hamilton Birchall*	144
Journey	*Edna St. Vincent Millay*	145
The Sojourner	*Sara Hamilton Birchall*	146
Traveller's Rest	*C. Fox-Smith*	147
Far From the Madding Crowd	*Nixon Waterman*	148
Streams	*Clinton Scollard*	149
The Call	*Edgar A. Guest*	150
The Road that Leads to Home	*Ethel E. Mannin*	150
Where Lies the Land?	*Arthur Hugh Clough*	151

Echoes from Vagabondia

Song of the Open Road	*Ogden Nash*	153
The Fiddling Lad	*Adelaide Crapsey*	154
Wanderthirst	*Gerald Gould*	155
The Vagabond	*Edgar A. Guest*	155
Gipsy Song	*Sara Hamilton Birchall*	156
The Road to Vagabondia	*Dana Burnet*	157
Gipsy Feet	*Fannie Stearns Davis*	158
A Strip of Blue	*Lucy Larcom*	160
Black Ashes	*Martha Haskell Clark*	161
The Wander Lure	*Kendall Banning*	162
Comrades of the Trail	*Mary Carolyn Davies*	163
The Vagrant	*Pauline Slender*	164
The Gipsy Wedding	*Sara Hamilton Birchall*	165
The Vagabond at Home	*Ruth Wright Kauffman*	165
The Gipsy Trail	*Rudyard Kipling*	166
St. Bartholomew's on the Hill	*Bliss Carman*	168
Fishing	*Edgar A. Guest*	169

❧ ❧ ❧ ❧ ❧ ❧ ❧ ❧ ❧ ❧ ❧ ❧ ❧ ❧ ❧ ❧ ❧ ❧ ❧ ❧ ❧ ❧ ❧ ❧

A Vagabond Song	*Bliss Carman*	171
Have You?	*Harry M. Dean*	171
Gipsy-Heart	*Katharine Lee Bates*	172
A More Ancient Mariner	*Bliss Carman*	173
Vagabonds	*Sara Hamilton Birchall*	175
The Gypsying	*Theodosia Garrison*	175
The Mendicants	*Bliss Carman*	176
The Beloved Vagabond	*W. G. Tinckom-Fernandez*	177
The Secret Voices	*Ethel E. Mannin*	178
The Pool	*Marjorie Pickthall*	179

The Turn of the Seasons

A Song of Early Autumn	*Richard Watson Gilder*	181
The Turn o' the Year	*Katherine Tynan*	183
April Music	*Clinton Scollard*	183
The Year's Awakening	*Thomas Hardy*	184
Spring's Answer	*Edwin Osgood Grover*	185
Morning Song	*Lancaster Pollard*	186
April Weather	*Bliss Carman*	186
The Runaway	*Cale Young Rice*	188
Spring Market	*Louise Driscoll*	189
Song in March	*Clinton Scollard*	190
Flower Chorus	*Ralph Waldo Emerson*	191
April's Coming	*Lancaster Pollard*	192
The Secret	*John Richard Moreland*	193
Spring	*Norman Gale*	193
April Weather	*Lizette Woodworth Reese*	194
Renewal	*Charles Hanson Towne*	195
April	*Theodosia Garrison*	195
The Immortal	*Cale Young Rice*	196
Spring	*Richard Hovey*	196
Blind	*Harry Kemp*	199
Spring Song	*Bliss Carman*	200
The Sweet Low Speech of the Rain	*Ella Higginson*	203
Early Spring	*Alfred Tennyson*	205
Spring	*Henry Timrod*	206
April, April	*William Watson*	208
April Rain	*Robert Loveman*	209
April	*Emily Dickinson*	210
April Morning	*George Elliston*	210
May-Lure	*Richard Burton*	211
Sunrise	*Robert Browning*	212
The Throstle	*Alfred Tennyson*	212
Tell All the World	*Harry Kemp*	213

Sorrow in a Garden	*May Riley Smith*	213
The Naturalist on a June Sunday	*Leonora Speyer*	215
Summer	*Richard Burton*	216
Autumn	*Emily Dickinson*	218
Overtones	*William Alexander Percy*	218
Carouse	*Charles Hanson Towne*	219
A Song in Autumn	*Theodosia Garrison*	219
An Autumn Garden	*Bliss Carman*	220
September	*Sara Hamilton Birchall*	223
Days Like These	*Ella Elizabeth Egbert*	224
Indian Summer	*Emily Dickinson*	225
The Deserted Pasture	*Bliss Carman*	226
The Coming of Dawn	*Grace Atherton Dennen*	227
Alms in Autumn	*Rose Fyleman*	228
November in England	*Thomas Hood*	228
The Hound	*Babette Deutsch*	229

Sky-Born Music

Evening in Tyringham Valley	*Richard Watson Gilder*	231
A Prairie Sunset	*E. J. Pratt*	232
Let Me Go Where'er I Will	*Ralph Waldo Emerson*	233
Pippa's Song	*Robert Browning*	233
The Whisper of Earth	*Edward J. O'Brien*	234
Sunrise	*Edgar A. Guest*	234
Prayer Before Poems	*Ann Blackwell Payne*	235
How Miracles Abound	*Clinton Scollard*	236
Little Things	*Orrick Johns*	236
Clouds and Sky	*Lancaster Pollard*	237
My Heart Leaps Up When I Behold	*William Wordsworth*	238
The Marshes	*Sidney Lanier*	238
Song	*John Vance Cheney*	239
Out-of-Doors	*Ethel E. Mannin*	239
The Whole Duty of Berkshire Brooks	*Grace Hazard Conkling*	240
A Word with a Skylark	*Sarah Piatt*	241
The Perilous Light	*Eva Gore-Booth*	241
Folly	*Vivian Yeiser Laramore*	243
One Blackbird	*Harold Monro*	243
A Rune of Riches	*Florence Converse*	244
The Picture	*Frederick O. Sylvester*	245
"Sic Vita"	*William Stanley Braithwaite*	245
A Blackbird Suddenly	*Joseph Auslander*	246
Credo	*Vera Wheatley*	247

Gospel of the Fields	*Arthur Upson*	247
The Welcome	*Arthur Powell*	248
Angels of the Spring	*Robert Stephen Hawkes*	249
God's World	*Edna St. Vincent Millay*	249
Rain	*Kenneth Slade Alling*	250
The Lark	*Lizette Woodworth Reese*	250
Farewell	*Harry Kemp*	251
The Comfort of the Stars	*Richard Burton*	251
The Last Hour	*Ethel Clifford*	252
Wasted Hours	*Medora Addison*	253
God is at the Anvil	*Lew Sarett*	253

At the End of the Trail

Time and Spirit	*Léonie Adams*	255
The Full Heart	*Robert Nichols*	256
That Time of Year	*William Shakespeare*	256
Hesperides	*Harry Kemp*	257
Changeless	*Martha Haskell Clark*	257
Homesick	*Julia C. R. Dorr*	258
If All the Skies	*Henry van Dyke*	259
"Gratias Ago"	*Geoffrey Howard*	260
Song of Ballyshannon	*Jeanne Robert Foster*	261
A Song of the Road	*Fred G. Bowles*	263
After Sunset	*Grace Hazard Conkling*	263
The Wanderer	*Zoe Akins*	264
The Trumpet of the Dawn	*Clinton Scollard*	265
Shared	*Lucy Larcom*	265
Up-Hill	*Christina Rossetti*	266
The Epitaph	*Katherine Tynan*	267
White Armour	*Jean Starr Untermeyer*	268
Shepherds Who Pastures Seek	*Herbert Trench*	268
Good-Bye	*Ralph Waldo Emerson*	270
The Day Is Done	*Henry Wadsworth Longfellow*	271
Memory	*Siegfried Sassoon*	272
Hark! Hark!	*Leonora Speyer*	273
The Noise of Leaves	*George Dillon*	273
Far in a Western Brookland	*A. E. Housman*	274
I Am Weary of Being Bitter	*Arthur Davison Ficke*	275
Death—Divination	*Charles Wharton Stork*	275
Thanks	*Norman Gale*	276
Index by Authors		277
Index by Titles		280
Index by First Lines		288

THE
NATURE LOVER'S
KNAPSACK

The Lure of the Road

In Spring-Time

THERE'S many a pool that holds a cloud
   Deep down for miles, to float along;
There's many a hedge that's white with may,
To bring the backward birds to song;
There's many a country lane that smells
   Of beanfields, through the night and day:
Then why should I be here this hour,
   In Spring-time, when the month is May?

There's nothing else but stone I see,
   With but this ribbon of a sky;
And not a garden big enough
   To share it with a butterfly.
Why do I walk these dull dark streets,
   In gloom and silence, all day long—
In Springtime, when the blackbird's day
   Is four and twenty hours of song?

W. H. Davies

I Must Out and Play Again

I MUST out and play again into the salt sea air!
And not be reading things in books and sitting in this chair.

I must run along the shore and laugh while yet there's time,
And find some woods to wander in and hills for me to climb.

I know where a fir tree gnarls itself into a seat
Above a lovely frog pond, green and gold beyond your feet.

I could find the muddy place where pink Mayflowers hide,
The clearing, burnt by fire, half way up the mountain side.

I could find where, if you listen, there's a Whippoorwill
Down where the fog is rising white and ominous and still.

I know where a mountain stream is made from little brooks—
Why should I be reading things that writers write in books?

What to me the towers made of nickels and of dimes?
I have seen a beech tree struck by lightning seven times!

Kathleen Millay

A Wanderer's Song

A WIND'S in the heart of me, a fire's in my heels,
I am tired of brick and stone and rumbling wagon-wheels;
I hunger for the sea's edge, the limits of the land,
Where the wild old Atlantic is shouting on the sand.

Oh, I'll be going, leaving the noises of the street,
To where a lifting foresail-foot is yanking at the sheet;
To a windy, tossing anchorage where yawls and ketches ride,
Oh, I'll be going, going, until I meet the tide.

And first I'll hear the sea-wind, the mewing of the gulls,
The clucking, sucking of the sea about the rusty hulls,
The songs at the capstan in the hooker warping out,
And then the heart of me'll know I'm there or thereabout.

Oh, I'm tired of brick and stone, the heart of me is sick,
For windy green, unquiet sea, the realm of Moby Dick;
And I'll be going, going, from the roaring of the wheels,
For a wind's in the heart of me, a fire's in my heels.
John Masefield

The Singer's Quest

I'VE been wandering, listening for a song,
Dreaming of a melody, all my life long. . . .
The lilting tune that God sang to rock the tides asleep,
And crooned above the cradled stars before they learned to creep.

Oh, there was laughter in it and many a merry chime,
Before He had turned moralist, grown old before His time,

And He was happy, trolling out His great blithe-hearted tune,
Before He slung the little earth beneath the sun and moon.

But I know that somewhere that song is rolling on,
Like flutes along the midnight, like trumpets in the dawn;
It throbs across the sunset and stirs the poplar tree
And rumbles in the long low thunder of the sea.

. . . .

First-love sang me one note and heart-break taught me two,
A child has told me three notes, and soon I'll know it through;
And when I stand before the Throne I'll hum it low and sly,
Watching for a great light of welcome in His eye, . . .

"Put a white raiment on him and a harp into his hand,
And golden sandals on his feet and tell the saints to stand
A little farther off unless they wish to hear the truth,
For this blessed lucky sinner is going to sing about my youth!"

Odell Shepard

The Toil of the Trail

WHAT have I gained by the toil of the trail?
    I know and know well.
I have found once again the lore I had lost
In the loud city's hell.

I have broadened my hand to the cinch and the axe,
I have laid my flesh to the rain;
I was hunter and trailer and guide;
I have touched the most primitive wildness again.

I have threaded the wild with the stealth of the deer,
No eagle is freer than I;
No mountain can thwart me, no torrent appall,
I defy the stern sky.
So long as I live these joys will remain,
I have touched the most primitive wildness again.

Hamlin Garland

Two Old Men

Sit-by-the-Fire:
>Men travel far and far away
>To come home on a happy day;
>And even they whom the roads call
>Who never know a home at all,
>They dream, I think, of roads that end
>At four walls with a fire and friend!

Foot-loose:
>I've never seen a hill but I
>Have dreamed a hill behind it,
>Nor ever watched a falling star
>Without the hope I'd find it,
>And all the islands of the sea
>Have known my name and called to me!

Sit-by-the-Fire:
>I have planted apple trees
>And eaten at my pleasure,
>My house is full of memories
>For an old man to treasure.
>This I have and that I have,
>And you may see them standing,
>Silver in the dining room,
>An old clock on the landing!

Foot-loose:
>I have neither house nor tree,
>Nor heirs alert and knowing,
>The four roads of eternity
>Are ways I would be going.
>Vagabonding in the skies
>I will not ask for Paradise!

Louise Driscoll

The Best Road of All

I LIKE a road that leads away to prospects white and fair,
A road that is an ordered road, like a nun's evening prayer;
But best of all I love a road that leads to God knows where.

You come upon it suddenly—you cannot seek it out;
It's like a secret still unheard and never noised about;
But when you see it, gone at once is every lurking doubt.

It winds beside some rushing stream where aspens lightly quiver;
It follows many a broken field by many a shining river;
It seems to lead you on and on, forever and forever!

You tramp along its dusty way beneath the shadowy trees,
And hear beside you chattering birds or happy booming bees,
And all around you golden sounds, the green leaves' litanies.

And here's a hedge and there's a cot; and then, strange, sudden turns—
A dip, a rise, a little glimpse where the red sunset burns;
A bit of sky at evening time, the scent of hidden ferns.

A winding road, a loitering road, the finger mark of God,
Traced when the Maker of the world leaned over ways untrod.
See! Here He smiled His glowing smile, and lo, the goldenrod!

I like a road that wanders straight; the King's highway is fair,
And lovely are the sheltered lanes that take you here and there;
But best of all I love a road that leads to God knows where.
Charles Hanson Towne

The Cry of the Dreamer

I AM tired of planning and toiling
   In the crowded hives of men,
Heart-weary of building and spoiling,
   And spoiling and building again,
And I long for the dear old river,
   Where I dreamed my youth away;
For a dreamer lives forever,
   And a toiler dies in a day.

I am sick of the showy seeming,
   Of life that is half a lie;
Of the faces lined with scheming
   In the throng that hurries by;
From the sleepless thought's endeavor
   I would go where the children play;
For a dreamer lives forever,
   And a thinker dies in a day.

I can feel no pride, but pity,
  For the burdens the rich endure;
There is nothing sweet in the city
  But the patient lives of the poor.
Oh, the little hands too skillful,
  And the child-mind choked with weeds!
The daughter's heart grown willful
  And the father's heart that bleeds!

No! No! from the streets' rude bustle,
  From trophies of mart and stage,
I would fly to the wood's low rustle
  And the meadows' kindly page.
Let me dream as of old by the river,
  And be loved for my dreams alway;
For a dreamer lives forever,
  And a toiler dies in a day.
                    John Boyle O'Reilly

Highways

WHO'S learned the lure of trodden ways,
    And walked them up and down,
May love a steeple in a mist,
  But cannot love a town.

Who's worn a bit of purple once
  Can never, never lie
All smothered in a little box
  When stars are in the sky.

Who's sipped old port in Venice glass
  May thirst for better brew—

He's drunk an amber wine of sun
And wet his mouth with dew!

Who's ground the grist of trodden ways—
　The gray dust and the brown—
May love red tiling two miles off—
　But cannot love a town.
Leslie Nelson Jennings

Afoot and Light-Hearted

AFOOT and light-hearted, I take to the open road,
　Healthy, free, the world before me,
The long brown path before me, leading wherever I choose.

Henceforth I ask not good-fortune—I myself am good-fortune;
Henceforth I whimper no more, postpone no more, need nothing,
Strong and content I travel the open road.
Walt Whitman

The Path That Leads To Nowhere

THERE'S a path that leads to Nowhere
　In a meadow that I know,
Where an inland island rises
　And the stream is still and slow;
There it wanders under willows
　And beneath the silver green

Of the birches' silent shadows
  Where the early violets lean.

Other pathways lead to Somewhere,
  But the one I love so well
Had no end and no beginning—
  Just the beauty of the dell,
Just the windflowers and the lilies
  Yellow striped as adder's tongue,
Seem to satisfy my pathway
  As it winds their sweets among.

There I go to meet the Springtime,
  When the meadow is aglow,
Marigolds amid the marshes,—
  And the stream is still and slow.—
There I find my fair oasis,
  And with care-free feet I tread
For the pathway leads to Nowhere,
  And the blue is overhead!

All the ways that lead to Somewhere
  Echo with the hurrying feet
Of the Struggling and the Striving,
  But the way I find so sweet
Bids me dream and bids me linger,
  Joy and Beauty are its goal,—
On the path that leads to Nowhere
  I have sometimes found my soul!
            Corinne Roosevelt Robinson

City-Weary

COME, let's get out of here! Out of the din of it,
  Out of the bickering, out of the sin of it,
Out of the smoke of it, out of the noise of it,

Out of the pitiful, lean, leering joys of it.
>Come on, let's go
>To a hilltop I know,
>Where the air is washed clean,
>And the trees are a-gleam
>With the gold of the sun,
>And there's naught to be done
>Save to lie there and look
>At life's beauties and dream.

Come, let's get out of here! Out of the stress of it,
Out of the paint and the powder and dress of it,
Out of the cry at the loss or the gain of it,
Out of the hurt and the grief and the pain of it.
>Let's slip away
>To the fields for a day,
>Where there is nothing
>On counters and shelves,
>Nothing to strive for,
>To work or contrive for,
>Let's leave the city
>And just be ourselves.

Come, let's get out of here! Out of the crush of it,
Out of the bedlam and out of the rush of it,
Out of the sham of it, out of the heat of it,
Out of the withering, scornful conceit of it.
>Come on! Let's go
>Where the clean breezes blow,
>Out where the splendors
>Are all that they seem;
>Let's merely walk awhile,
>Ponder and talk awhile,
>Giving our souls
>The full sweep of a dream.

Edgar A. Guest

The Faun

I WILL go out to grass with that old King,
For I am weary of clothes and cooks.
I long to paddle with the throats of brooks,
To lie down with the clover
Tickling me all over,
And watch the boughs above me sway and swing.
Come, I will pluck off custom's livery,
Nor longer be a lackey to old Time.
Time shall serve me, and at my feet shall fling
The spoil of listless minutes. I shall climb
The wild trees for my food, and run
Through dale and upland as a fox runs free,
Laugh for cool joy and sleep i' the warm sun,—
And men will call me mad, like that old King.

For I am woodland-nurtur'd, and have made
Dryads my bedfellows,
And I have played
With the sleek Naiads in the splash of pools
And made a mock of gowned and trousered fools.
And I am half Faun now, and my heart goes
Out to the forest and the crack of twigs,
The drip of wet leaves, and the low soft laughter
Of brooks that chuckle o'er old mossy jests
And sáy them over to themselves, the nests
Of squirrels, and the holes the chipmunk digs,
Where through the branches the slant rays
Dapple with sunlight the leaf-matted ground,
And th' wind comes with blown vesture rustling after,
And through the woven lattice of crisp sound
A bird's song lightens like a maiden's face.

Oh, goodly damp smell of the ground!
Oh, rough sweet bark of the trees!

Oh, clear sharp cracklings of sound!
Oh, life that's a-thrill and a-bound
With the vigor of boyhood and morning and the noontide's rapture of ease!
Was there ever a weary heart in the world?
A lag in the body's urge, or a flag of the spirit's wing?
Did a man's heart ever break
For a lost hope's sake?
For here there is lilt in the quiet and calm in the quiver of things.
Ay, this old oak, gray-grown and knurled,
Solemn and sturdy and big,
Is as young of heart, as alert and elate in his rest,
As the oriole there that clings to the tip of the twig
And scolds at the wind that it buffets too rudely his nest.
Richard Hovey

The Call of the Wild[1]

HAVE you gazed on naked grandeur where there's nothing else to gaze on,
  Set pieces and drop-curtain scenes galore,
Big mountains heaved to heaven, which the blinding sunsets blazon,
  Black canyons where the rapids rip and roar?
Have you swept the visioned valley with the green stream streaking through it,
  Searched the Vastness for a something you have lost?
Have you strung your soul to silence? Then for God's sake go and do it;
  Hear the challenge, learn the lesson, pay the cost.

[1] From "The Spell of the Yukon and Other Verses" by Robert W Service. Copyright by Barse & Hopkins, Newark, N. J.

Have you wandered in the wilderness, the sage-brush desolation,
  The bunch-grass levels where the cattle graze?
Have you whistled bits of rag-time at the end of all creation,
  And learned to know the desert's little ways?
Have you camped upon the foothills, have you galloped o'er the ranges,
  Have you roamed the arid sun-lands through and through?
Have you chummed up with the mesa? Do you know its moods and changes?
  Then listen to the wild—it's calling you.

Have you known the Great White Silence, not a snow-gemmed twig aquiver?
  (Eternal truths that shame our soothing lies.)
Have you broken trail on snowshoes? mushed your huskies up the river,
  Dared the unknown, led the way, and clutched the prize?
Have you marked the map's void spaces, mingled with the mongrel races,
  Felt the savage strength of brute in every thew?
And though grim as hell the worst is, can you round it off with curses?
  Then hearken to the Wild—it's wanting you.

Have you suffered, starved and triumphed, grovelled down, yet grasped at glory,
  Grown bigger in the bigness of the whole?
"Done things" just for the doing, letting babblers tell the story,
  Seeing through the nice veneer the naked soul?
Have you seen God in His splendors, heard the text that nature renders?
  (You'll never hear it in the family pew.)

The simple things, the true things, the silent men who do
    things—
  Then listen to the Wild,—it's calling you.

They have cradled you in custom, they have primed you with
    their preaching,
  They have soaked you in convention through and through;
They have put you in a showcase; you're a credit to their
    teaching—
  But can't you hear the Wild?—it's calling you.
Let us probe the silent places, let us seek what luck betide
    us;
  Let us journey to a lonely land I know.
There's a whisper on the night-wind, there's a star agleam
    to guide us,
  And the Wild is calling, calling . . . let us go.
                                      Robert W. Service

A City Voice

OUTSIDE here in the city the burning pavements lie,
  There's heat and grime and blown black dust to help
    the day go by,
  There's the groaning of the city like a goaded, beaten
    beast;—
I know a place where God's great trees go up to meet His
    sky—
  Like an army green with banners, and a happy wind re-
    leased,
Goes swinging like a merry child among the branches high.

Outside here in the city there's a poison in the air—

The fevered, heavy hand o' heat that smites and may not
    spare;
  There's little comfort in the night—there's torment in the
    day;—
I know a place where cool and deep the quiet lake lies bare,
  All day about its shaded brink the wild birds dart and
    play,
And willows dip their finger-tips like dainty ladies there.

Oh, the heart of me is hungering for my own, own place!
I'm tortured with the slaying heat, the dizzy headrace.
  Oh, for the soft, cold touch of grass about my tired feet,
The breath of pine and cedar blown against my weary face,
  The lip-lap of the water like a little song and sweet,
And God's green trees and God's blue skies above me for
    a space.

Theodosia Garrison

Fishing

A DAY to dream
  Along a stream,
The song of birds
Instead of words,
And pictures rare
Flung everywhere.

Instead of smoke
To blind and choke,
An atmosphere
That's sweet and clear,
The trees instead
Of chimneys red.

A patch of sky
To rest the eye;
Instead of noise,
A thousand joys;
Instead of greed,
A kindlier creed.

A day to dream
Along the stream,
To think and plan,
Restores a man,
And this he knows
Who fishing goes.

Edgar A. Guest

Camping Song

Has your dinner lost its savor?
  Has your greeting lost its cheer?
Is your daily stunt a burden?
  Is your laughter half a sneer?
There's a medicine to cure you,
  There's a way to lift your load,
With a horse and a saddle and a mile of open road.

Is your eyeball growing bilious?
  Is your temper getting short?
Is this life a blind delusion,
  Or a grim, unlovely sport?
There's a world of health and beauty,
  There's a help that cannot fail,
In a day behind the burros
  On a dusty mountain trail.

Come out, old man, we're going
  To a land that's free and large,
Where the rainless skies are resting
  On a snowy mountain marge.
When we camp in God's own country,
  You will find yourself again,
With a fire and a blanket and the stars upon the plain!
                    Bliss Carman

The Green Inn

THE roof is high and arched and blue,
  The floor is spread with pine;
On my four walls the sunlight falls
  In golden flecks and fine;
And swift and fleet on noiseless feet
  The Four Winds bring me wine.

Here none may mock an empty purse
  Or ragged coat and poor,
But Silence waits within the gates,
  And Peace beside the door;
The weary guest is welcomest,
  The richest pays no score.

.   .   .   .

Oh, you who in the House of Strife
  Quarrel and game and sin,
Come out and see what cheer may be
  For starveling souls and thin
Who come at last from drought and fast
  To sit in God's Green Inn.

                    Theodosia Garrison

Wanderlust

THE highways and the byways, the kind sky folding all,
And never a care to drag me back and never a voice to call;
Only the call of the long white road to the far horizon's wall.

The glad seas and the mad seas, the seas on a night of June,
And never a hand to beckon back from the path of the new-lit moon;
Never a night that lasts too long or a dawn that breaks too soon!

The shrill breeze and the hill breeze, the sea breeze fierce and bold,
And never a breeze that gives the lie to a tale that a breeze has told;
Always the tale of the strange and new in the countries strange and old.

Isabel Ecclestone Mackay

Song[1]

SOMETHING calls and whispers, along the city street,
Through shrill cries of children and soft stir of feet,
And makes my blood to quicken and makes my flesh to pine.
The mountains are calling; the winds wake the pine.

Past the quivering poplars that tell of water near
The long road is sleeping, the white road is clear.

[1] From "The Way of Perfect Love."

Yet scent and touch can summon, afar from brook and tree,
The deep boom of surges, the gray waste of sea.

Sweet to dream and linger, in windless orchard close,
On bright brows of ladies to garland the rose,
But all the time are glowing, beyond this little world,
The still light of planets and the star-swarms whirled.
Georgiana Goddard King

In City Streets

YONDER in the heather there's a bed for sleeping,
   Drink for one athirst, ripe blackberries to eat;
Yonder in the sun the merry hares go leaping,
   And the pool is clear for travel-wearied feet.
Sorely throb my feet, a-tramping London highways,
   (Ah! the springy moss upon a northern moor!)
Through the endless streets, the gloomy squares and byways,
   Homeless in the City, poor among the poor!

London streets are gold—ah, give me leaves a-glinting
   'Midst grey dykes and hedges in the autumn sun!
London water's wine, poured out for all unstinting—
   God! For the little brooks that tumble as they run!

Oh, my heart is fain to hear the soft wind blowing,
   Soughing through the fir-tops up on northern fells!
Oh, my eye's an ache to see the brown burns flowing
   Through the peaty soil and tinkling heatherbells.
Ada Smith

"Up! Up! My Friend, And Quit Your Books"

UP! up! my Friend, and quit your books;
  Or surely you'll grow double:
Up! up! my Friend, and clear your looks;
Why all this toil and trouble?

The sun, above the mountain's head,
A freshening lustre mellow
Through all the long green fields has spread,
His first sweet evening yellow.

Books! 'tis a dull and endless strife:
Come, hear the woodland linnet,
How sweet his music! on my life,
There's more of wisdom in it.

And hark! how blithe the throstle sings,
He, too, is no mean preacher:
Come forth into the light of things,
Let Nature be your Teacher.

She has a world of ready wealth,
Our minds and hearts to bless—
Spontaneous wisdom breathed by health,
Truth breathed by cheerfulness.

One impulse from a vernal wood
May teach you more of man,
Of moral evil and of good,
Than all the sages can.

Sweet is the lore which Nature brings;
Our meddling intellect

Misshapes the beauteous forms of things:—
We murder to dissect.

Enough of Science and of Art;
Close up these barren leaves;
Come forth, and bring with you a heart
That watches and receives.

William Wordsworth

Road Song

IT'S home for me and a snug roof-tree
　When frosts hold the earth in thrall,
But it's hey, I say, for the broad highway,
When the young year's voices call.
'Tis then I would be rolling off,
A-bowling off, a-strolling off—
An errant leaf bound whitherward
The wind of fancy wills;
'Tis then I would be going off,
A-whirling off, a-blowing off
Along the road that leads away
Beyond the purple hills.

'Twas hearth and home when the sky's gray dome
Hung low and the north wind skirled;
Now it's hey for the reel of the out-bound keel,
And it's ho for the great round world.
'Tis now I would be roving off
A-shoving off, a-moving off
To where the far horizon shows
Mysterious and dim;
It's time that I was shipping off

A-rising and a-dipping off
To strange and unknown ports that lie
Below the round world's rim.

Oh, some were made for peaceful shade
Of their vine and their own fig tree,
But marked of fate with the gipsy trait,
It's the open road for me.
And so I would be pushing on,
A-trekking on, a-mushing on,
And leave the old well-trodden trails
Long merry miles behind.
'Tis joyful I'd go swinging off,
A-whooping and a-singing off,
As goal-less as a vagrant crow
A-winging down the wind.

James Stuart Montgomery

Walking at Night

MY face is wet with the rain
But my heart is warm to the core,
For I follow at will again
The road that I loved of yore;
And the dim trees beat the dark,
And the swelling ditches moan,
But my heart is a singing, soaring lark
For I travel the road alone.
Alone in the living night
Away from the babble of tongues;
Alone with the old delight
Of the night wind in my lungs;
And the wet air on my cheeks

And the warm blood in my veins,
Alone with the joy he knows who seeks
The thresh of the young spring rains,
With the smell of the pelted earth,
The tearful drip of the trees,
Making him dream of the sound of mirth
That comes with the clearing breeze.
'Tis a rare and wondrous sight
To tramp the wet awhile
And watch the slow delight
Of the sun's first pallid smile,
And hear the meadows breathe again
And see the far woods turn green,
Drunk with the glory of wind and rain
And the sun's warm smile between!
I have made me a vagrant song,
For my heart is warm to the core,
And I'm glad, oh, glad that the night is long
For I travel the road once more.
And the dim trees beat the dark
And the swelling ditches moan,
With the joy of the singing, soaring lark
I travel the road, alone!

Amory Hare

Road Song

GIVE me the clear blue sky overhead, and the long road to my feet,
And the winds of heaven to winnow me through, and a brother tramp to greet,
With an Inn at the end of day for rest, and the world may keep its bays—

For these are the gifts of the wayside gods, and the gifts
    that I would praise.

Come from the murk of your city streets to the tent of all
    the world,
When your final word on Art is said, and your flag of Faith
    is furled,
When your heart no longer gives a throb at the first faint
    breath of Spring—
Ah, turn your feet to the ribbon-road with a chorus all
    may sing!

. . . .

Then give me the clear blue sky overhead, and the long road
    to my feet,
And a dog to tell my secrets to, and a brother tramp to
    meet—
And the years may take their toll of me till I come to the
    weary West,
And I lodge for good in the world's own Inn, a wayworn,
    waiting guest!

W. G. Tinckom-Fernandez

A Song of the Open Road

THE old Earth-Mother calls us,
    And we hearken unto her cry,
For we dare not question her bidding
    Lest we sicken and droop and die.
The spirit of change is burning
    As a fever in heart and brain.
In the ranks of the Free Companions
    We must take to the road again.

We have lain in the tents of the dwellers;
  We have ta'en of their drink and food;
We, that were weary, have slumbered,
  Have slumbered and found rest good.
We have kissed the lips of their maidens,
  From their kin we have chosen our brides;
But the summons has come from the Mother,
  And no one who hears it abides.

We do the will of the Mother,
  We bow to the Word she sends,
Though we know not whither we journey,
  Nor the goal where the journey ends.
On the quest of the Strange Adventure
  We sally, hand-in-hand,
As the men of the days nomadic
  When the hunter was lord in the land.

The winds a-sweep through the forests
  Shall brace our souls for the march,
The balm of the dews descending
  Shall chasten the heats that parch.
Through vista of brakes entangled
  The stars shall guide, in the night,
By day the sun shall quicken
  The pulse of our life's delight

Ho! for the zest of travel,
  The wayfarer's romance,
The joy of the unexpected,
  The hope of the noble chance.
We have girded our feet with sandals,
  We carry the pilgrim's load.
In the ranks of the Free Companions
  We take to the open road.

Louis J. McQuilland

A Maine Trail

COME follow, heart upon your sleeve,
    The trail, a-teasing by,
Past tasseled corn and fresh-mown hay,
    Trim barns and farm-house shy,
Past hollyhocks and white well-sweep,
    Through pastures bare and wild,
Oh come, let's fare to the heart-o'-the-wood
    With the faith of a little child.

Strike in by the gnarled way through the swamp
    Where late the laurel shone,
An intimate close where you meet yourself
    And come unto your own,
By bouldered brook to the hidden spring
    Where breath of ferns blows sweet
And swift birds break the silence as
    Their shadows cross your feet.

Stout-hearted thrust through gold-green copse
    To garner the woodland glee,
To weave a garment of warm delight,
    Of sun-spun ecstasy;
'Twill shield you all winter from frosty eyes,
    'Twill shield your heart from cold;
Such greens!—how the Lord Himself loves green!
    Such sun!—how He loves the gold!

Then on till flaming fireweed
    Is quenched in forest deep;
Tread soft! The sumptuous paven moss
    Is spread for Dryads' sleep;
And list ten thousand thousand spruce
    Lift up their voice to God—

We can a little understand,
   Born of the self-same sod.

Oh, come, the welcoming trees lead on,
   Their guests are we to-day;
Shy violets smile, proud branches bow,
   Gay mushrooms mark the way;
The silence is a courtesy,
   The well-bred calm of kings;
Come haste! the hour sets its face
   Unto great Happenings.

Gertrude Huntington McGiffert

The Spell of the Pool

THERE'S a crystal-arrowed riffle at the turning of the river,
   There's a waterfall where nature teaches school,
There's a bank of swaying alder with each budding twig aquiver—
   And there's magic in the murmur of the pool!

Can't you see the cold, blue water as it eddies, sparkles, flashes
   In the willow-shadowed reaches of the stream,
And the ever-widening ripples where the trout, in falling, splashes
   As the osprey drops his quarry with a scream?

L. Burton Crane, Jr.

The Lake

THERE is a lake—but I forget its name,
That flickers in my memory like flame!

Guarded by Dolomites whose magic glow
Of red primeval merges into snow.

A lake so beautiful, God gave it birth
By melting one vast emerald on earth!

A lake so strange, that, did its waters part,
Undine would be enshrined within its heart.

And as with lovely sound the air may fill,
Though chords are hushed and all the strings be still,

So will this lake—but I forget its name—
Flicker within my memory like flame!
Eleanour Norton

The Great Outdoors

O GREAT outdoors, without floors,
Or walls, or roofs, or bounds,
Grant this day that I may stray
Amidst thy plains and mounds,
Let me be among the free
That climb thy purple hills;
Let me breathe the scents that wreathe
Thy violet bordered rills:
Let thy sun, till day be done,

Shine from out thy great blue sky;
Let thy starlight and the still night
Soothe my rest when down I lie;
Let the shadows cool the meadows,
And the night sounds whisper low,
In the stillness of thy valleys
Where the waters lap and flow.

Maud Russell

Come, Spur Away!

COME, spur away,
   I have no patience for a longer stay,
    But must go down
And leave the chargeable noise of this great town:
    I will the country see,
    Where old simplicity,
      Though hid in gray,
      Doth look more gay
Than foppery in plush and scarlet clad.
  Farewell, you city wits, that are
    Almost at civil war—
'Tis time that I grow wise, when all the world grows mad.

. . . .

    Ours is the sky,
Where at what fowl we please our hawk shall fly:
    Nor will we spare
To hunt the crafty fox or timorous hare;
    But let our hounds run loose
    In any ground they'll choose;
      The buck shall fall,
      The stag, and all.

Our pleasures must from their own warrants be,
   For to my Muse, if not to me,
     I'm sure all game is free:
Heaven, earth, are all but parts of her great royalty.
                              Thomas Randolph

Hunting Song

OH, who would stay indoor, indoor,
   When the horn is on the hill? (*Bugle:* Tarantara!)
With the crisp air stinging, and the huntsmen singing,
And a ten-tined buck to kill!

Before the sun goes down, goes down,
We shall slay the buck of ten; (*Bugle:* Tarantara!)
And the priest shall say benison, and we shall ha'e venison,
When we come home again.

Let him that loves his ease, his ease,
Keep close and house him fair; (*Bugle:* Tarantara!)
We'll still be a stranger to the merry thrill of danger
And the joy of the open air.

But he that loves the hills, the hills,
Let him come out to-day! (*Bugle:* Tarantara!)
For the horses are neighing, and the hounds are baying,
And the hunt's up, and away!
                              Richard Hovey

The Call

HAVE you heard the calling, calling, of the Distance,
   Through the purple reaches where the mountains wait;
With Dreamland round their shoulders, where the sunset
   fire smoulders—
   Oh, the guarding Distance calls us from their gate.

In the morning it entices with the sunrise,
   In the evening it is urging through the gold;
We must heed the sweet insistence, for this mystic blue-veiled Distance
   Hides our wished-for land of Dreams within its hold.

We will cinch the saddle tighter, tie the strings of wide sombrero,
   While the mists about the top are gray and dim;
With the eager trail uptrending, and the morning sky low bending—
   Oh, the evening star will we see o'er the rim.

When the wind blows thin and keen about the summit,
   And the camp-fire sparkles warm upon the brim,
On a couch of pine boughs fragrant, who would scorn to be a vagrant,
   And follow when the Distance calls to him?

Cora D. Fenton

The King's Highway

"El Camino Real"

ALL in the golden weather, forth let us ride to-day,
   You and I together, on the King's Highway,
The blue skies above us, and below the shining sea;
There's many a road to travel, but it's this road for me.

It's a long road and sunny, and the fairest in the world—
There are peaks that rise above it in their snowy mantles curled,

And it leads from the mountains through a hedge of chaparral,
Down to the waters where the sea gulls call.

It's a long road and sunny, it's a long road and old,
And the brown padres made it for the flocks of the fold;
They made it for the sandals of the sinner-fold that trod
From the fields in the open to the shelter-house of God.

They made it for the sandals of the sinner-fold of old;
Now the flocks they are scattered and death keeps the fold;
But you and I together we will take the road to-day,
With the breath in our nostrils, on the King's Highway.

We will take the road together through the morning's golden glow,
And we'll dream of those who trod it in the mellowed long ago;
We will stop at the Missions where the sleeping padres lay,
And we'll bend a knee above them for their souls' sake to pray.

We'll ride through the valleys where the blossom's on the tree,
Through the orchards and the meadows with the bird and the bee,
And we'll take the rising hills where the manzanitas grow,
Past the gray tails of waterfalls where blue violets blow.

Old Conquistadores, oh, brown priests and all,
Give us your ghosts for company when night begins to fall;

There's many a road to travel, but it's this road to-day,
With the breath of God about us on the King's Highway.
John Steven McGroarty

God Made This Day Fer Me

JES' the sort o' weather and jes' the sort o' sky
  Which seem to suit my fancy, with the white clouds driftin' by
On a sea o' smooth blue water. Oh, I ain't an egotist,
With an "I" in all my thinkin', but I'm willin' to insist
That the Lord that made us humans and the birds in every tree
Knows my special sort o' weather an' He made this day fer me.

This is jes' my style o' weather—sunshine floodin' all the place,
An' the breezes from the eastward blowin' gently on my face.
An' the woods chock-full o' singin' till you'd think birds never had
A single care to fret 'em or a grief to make 'em sad.
Oh, I settle down contented in the shadow of a tree,
An' tell myself right proudly that the day was made fer me.

It's my day, sky an' sunshine, an' the temper o' the breeze,
Here's the weather I would fashion could I run things as I please—
Beauty dancin' all around me, music ringin' everywhere,
Like a weddin' celebration. Why I've plumb fergot my care

An' the tasks I should be doin' fer the rainy days to be
While I'm huggin' the delusion that God made this day
    fer me.
                                                  Edgar A. Guest

The Country Faith

HERE in the country's heart
   Where the grass is green
Life is the same sweet life
As it e'er hath been.

Trust in a God still lives,
   And the bell at morn
Floats with a thought of God
O'er the rising corn.

God comes down in the rain,
   And the crop grows tall—
This is the country faith,
   And the best of all!
                        Norman Gale

Yellow Warblers

THE first faint dawn was flushing up the skies
   When, dreamland still bewildering mine eyes,
I looked out to the oak that, winter-long,
—a winter wild with war and woe and wrong—
Beyond my casement had been void of song.

And lo! with golden buds the twigs were set,
Live buds that warbled like a rivulet
Beneath a veil of willows. Then I knew
Those tiny voices, clear as drops of dew,
Those flying daffodils that fleck the blue,

Those sparkling visitants from myrtle isles,
Wee pilgrims of the sun, that measure miles
Innumerable over land and sea
With wings of shining inches. Flakes of glee,
They filled that dark old oak with jubilee,

Foretelling in delicious roundelays
Their dainty courtships on the dipping sprays,
How they should fashion nests, mate helping mate,
Of milkweed flax and fern-down delicate
To keep sky-tinted eggs inviolate.

Listening to those blithe notes, I slipped once more
From lyric dawn through dreamland's open door,
And there was God, Eternal Life that sings,
Eternal joy, brooding all mortal things,
A nest of stars, beneath untroubled wings.

Katharine Lee Bates

Reveille

WHAT sudden bugle calls us in the night
    And wakes us from a dream that we had shaped;
Flinging us sharply up against a fight
    We thought we had escaped.

It is no easy waking, and we win
    No final peace; our victories are few.
But still imperative forces pull us in
    And sweep us somehow through.

Summoned by a supreme and confident power
    That wakes our sleeping courage like a blow,
We rise, half-shaken, to the challenging hour,
    And answer it—and go.

Louis Untermeyer

Growing Things

The Mangroves Dance

THE mangroves dance in the light of the moon,
  Three feet, four feet,
More feet, many feet.
Dance and prance in the light of the moon,
Dance and prance to the swishing tune
Of wind on the waves, in the light of the moon.

Gnarled old mangroves, bent and marred,
With crooked arms—
With bodies scarred by wind and wave,
When the sea mounts high, and through the sky
The tearing storm goes shrieking by.

Gray old mangroves,
Awkward, stumbling,
Twisted legs—tortuous—tumbling—
To a shuffling tune,
As they dance and prance in the light of the moon.

The mangroves dance in the light of the moon,
Dance in a trance as the tide mounts high,
And only the moon in the southern sky,
Can see them groping, prancing by,
Three feet, four feet,
More feet, many feet.
Can hear the drone of the muffled tune,
As the mangroves dance in the light of the moon.
                                    Rose Strong Hubbell

Who Plants a Dogwood Tree

WHO plants a dogwood tree holds hands with God,
　　And shares one smallest part of His design;
Who visions beauty from the altered sod
Employs His method, sets His stake and line.
For beauty triumphs in God's scheme for earth
Where eager tendrils heal a barren place,
Where root and blade attack, and strange rebirth
Transfigures ugliness of form to grace.
Scarce any virtue can attain this goal:
A glowing partner-concept of His plan,
A wisdom that discerns the strength of soul
That beauty's fire engenders in a man.
He works with God for all posterity
Who spades the earth to plant a dogwood tree.
                                    Mabel Brown

Afoot

COMES the lure of green things growing,
Comes the call of waters flowing—
And the wayfarer desire
Moves and wakes and would be going.

Hark the migrant hosts of June
Marching nearer noon by noon!
Hark the gossip of the grasses
Bivouacked beneath the moon!

Long the quest and far the ending
When my wayfarer is wending—
When desire is once afoot,
Doom behind and dream attending!

In his ears the phantom chime
Of incommunicable rhyme,
He shall chase the fleeting camp-fires
Of the Bedouins of Time.

Farer by uncharted ways,
Dumb as death to plaint or praise,
Unreturning he shall journey,
Fellow to the nights and days;

Till upon the outer bar
Stilled the moaning currents are,
Till the flame achieves the zenith,
Till the moth attains the star,

Till through laughter and through tears
Fair the final peace appears,

And about the watered pastures
Sink to sleep the nomad years!

Charles G. D. Roberts

Grace for Gardens

LORD God in Paradise,
   Look upon our sowing,
Bless the little gardens
   And the good green growing!
Give us sun,
   Give us rain,
Bless the orchards
   And the grain!

Lord God in Paradise,
   Please bless the beans and peas,
Give us corn full on the ear—
   We will praise Thee, Lord, for these!
Bless the blossom
   And the root,
Bless the seed
   And the fruit!

Lord God in Paradise,
   Over my brown field is seen,
Trembling and adventuring,
   A miracle of green.
Send such grace
   As you know,
To keep it safe
   And make it grow!

Lord God in Paradise,
   For the wonder of the seed,
Wondering, we praise you, while
   We tell you of our need.
Look down from Paradise,
   Look upon our sowing,
Bless the little gardens
   And the good green growing!
Give us sun,
   Give us rain,
Bless the orchards
   And the grain!

Louise Driscoll

My Garden

A GARDEN is a lovesome thing, Got wot!
   Rose plot,
Fringed pool,
Ferned grot—
The veriest school
Of peace; and yet the fool
Contends that God is not—
Not God! in gardens! when the eve is cool!
Nay, but I have a sign;
'Tis very sure God walks in mine.

Thomas E. Brown

April

THE charm is working, now,
   On the alder bough;
Odors are afloat;

The brook has a new note;
Nightly in the silence grow
Murmurs only lovers know,—
Love's own minstrelsy
Beginning in the tree;
The airy hammers of the rain
Tap—are still again.

John Vance Cheney

A Song the Grass Sings

THE violet is much too shy,
    The rose too little so;
I think I'll ask the buttercup
    If I may be her beau.

When winds go by, I'll nod to her
    And she will nod to me,
And I will kiss her on the cheek
    As gently as may be.

And when the mower cuts us down,
    Together we will pass,
I smiling at the buttercup,
    She smiling at the grass.

Charles G. Blanden

The Young Dandelion

I AM a bold fellow
    As ever was seen,
With my shield of yellow,
    In the grass green.

You may uproot me
  From field and from lane,
Trample me, cull me—
  I spring up again.

I never flinch, sir,
  Wherever I dwell,
Give me an inch, sir,
  I'll soon take an ell.

Drive me from garden,
  In anger and pride,
I'll thrive and harden
  By the roadside.
                    Dinah Mulock Craik

Sunflowers

MY tall sunflowers love the sun,
    Love the burning August noons
When the locust tunes its viol,
  And the cricket croons.

When the purple night draws on,
  With its planets hung on high,
And the attared winds of slumber
  Wander down the sky.

Still my sunflowers love the sun,
  Keep their ward and watch and wait
Till the rosy key of morning
  Opes the eastern gate.

Then, when they have deeply quaffed
  From the brimming cups of dew,

You can hear their golden laughter
All the garden through!

Clinton Scollard

Wishing

RING-TING! I wish I were a primrose,
   A bright yellow primrose, blooming in the spring!
  The stooping boughs above me,
  The wandering bee to love me,
The ferns and moss to creep across,
And the elm-tree for our king!

Nay—stay! I wish I were an elm-tree,
A great, lofty elm-tree, with green leaves gay!
  The winds would set them dancing,
  The sun and moonshine glance in,
The birds would house among the boughs,
And ever sweetly sing!

Oh—no! I wish I were a robin,
A robin or a little wren, everywhere to go;
  Through forest, field, or garden,
  And ask no leave or pardon,
Till winter comes with icy thumbs
To ruffle up our wings!

William Allingham

Rain

IS it raining, little flower?—
  Be glad of rain!
Too much sun would wither thee;
  'Twill shine again.

The sky is very black, 'tis true;
But just behind it shines the blue.

God watches; and thou wilt have sun,
When clouds their perfect work have done.
Lucy Larcom

To the Dandelion

DEAR common flower, that grow'st beside the way,
   Fringing the dusty road with harmless gold,
  First pledge of blithesome May,
Which children pluck, and, full of pride uphold,
  High-hearted buccaneers, o'erjoyed that they
An Eldorado in the grass have found,
Which not the rich earth's ample round
May match in wealth, thou art more dear to me
Than all the prouder summer-blooms may be.

Gold such as thine ne'er drew the Spanish prow
Through the primeval hush of Indian seas,
  Nor wrinkled the lean brow
Of age, to rob the lover's heart of ease;
  'Tis the Spring's largess, which she scatters now
To rich and poor alike, with lavish hand,
Though most hearts never understand
To take it at God's value, but pass by
The offered wealth with unrewarded eye.

Thou art my tropics and mine Italy;
To look at thee unlocks a warmer clime;
  The eyes thou givest me
Are in the heart, and heed not space or time:
  Not in mid June the golden-cuirassed bee

Feels a more summer-like warm ravishment
In the white lily's breezy tent,
His fragrant Sybaris, than I, when first
From the dark green thy yellow circles burst.

Then think I of deep shadows on the grass,
Of meadows where in sun the cattle graze,
  Where, as the breezes pass,
The gleaming rushes lean a thousand ways,
  Of leaves that slumber in a cloudy mass,
Or whiten in the wind, of waters blue
That from the distance sparkle through
Some woodland gap, and of a sky above,
Where one white cloud like a stray lamb doth move.

My childhood's earliest thoughts are linked with thee;
The sight of thee calls back the robin's song,
  Who, from the dark old tree
Beside the door, sang clearly all day long,
  And I, secure in childish piety,
Listened as if I heard an angel sing
With news from heaven, which he could bring
Fresh every day to my untainted ears
When birds and flowers and I were happy peers.

How like a prodigal doth nature seem,
When thou, for all thy gold, so common art!
  Thou teachest me to deem
More sacredly of every human heart,
  Since each reflects in joy its scanty gleam
Of heaven, and could some wondrous secret show,
Did we but pay the love we owe,
And with a child's undoubting wisdom look
On all these living pages of God's book.

James Russell Lowell

The Grass

A CHILD said *What is the grass?* fetching it to me
    with full hands;
How could I answer the child? I do not know what it is
    any more than he.

I guess it must be the flag of my disposition, out of hopeful
    green stuff woven.

Or I guess it is the handkerchief of the Lord,
A scented gift and remembrancer designedly dropt,
Bearing the owner's name someway in the corners, that
    we may see and remark, and say *Whose?*
                                                    Walt Whitman

Buttercups

THERE must be fairy miners
    Just underneath the mould,
Such wondrous quaint designers
    Who live in caves of gold.

They take the shining metals,
    And beat them into shreds;
And mould them into petals,
    To make the flowers' heads.

Sometimes they melt the flowers
    To tiny seeds like pearls,
And store them up in bowers
    For little boys and girls.

And still a tiny fan turns
 Above a forge of gold,
To keep, with fairy lanterns,
 The world from growing old.
Wilfrid C. Thorley

The Lilac

WHO thought of the lilac?
 "I," dew said,
"I made up the lilac
out of my head."

"She made up the lilac!
Pooh!" thrilled a linnet,
and each dew-note had a
lilac in it.

Humbert Wolfe

The Hollyhocks

THE hollyhocks are standing
 In groups against the wall,
Engaged in conversation
With the lowly flowers small,
That gaze with admiration
On floral dames so gay,
Who wear such ruffled bonnets
Of crimson deep to-day.

. . . . . .

The wind has paused to listen
To the dames of high degree,

And the mignonette and pansies
Are laughing with such glee!
The mullein pinks are blushing,
And the poppies say, "Oh, see,
In the dame's gay frilled red bonnet
She has a bumblebee!"

Ray Laurance

The Ragged Regiment

I LOVE the ragged veterans of June,
Not your trim troop drill-marshalled for display
In gardens fine,—but such as dare the noon
With saucy faces by the public way.

Moth-mullein, with its moth-wing petals white,
Round Dandelion, and flouncing Bouncing-Bet,
The golden Butter-and-Eggs, and Ox-eye bright,
Wild Parsley, and tall Milkweed bee-beset.

Ha, sturdy tramps of Nature, mustered out
From garden service, scorned and set apart,—
There's not one member of your ragged rout
But makes a warmth of welcome in my heart.

Alice Williams Brotherton

Marigolds

THE marigolds are nodding:
I wonder what they know.
Go, listen very gently;
You may persuade them so.

Go, be their little brother,
As humble as the grass,
And lean upon the hill-wind,
And watch the shadows pass.

Put off the pride of knowledge,
Put by the fear of pain;
You may be counted worthy
To live with them again.

Be Darwin in your patience,
Be Chaucer in your love;
They may relent and tell you
What they are thinking of.

Bliss Carman

In a Garden

SKY!
Why are you so very gay
To-day?
Dimpled with the clouds at play,
Blithe with the sun's vivacious ray . . .
Why?

Moon!
Why do you pursue me so?
Are you whispering
That youth passes over-soon?
Don't you know
I've buried you a dozen times
Behind tall buildings?—Pagan thing!
The very Churches clutch at you

With grasping spires
To tear you from the sky!
Veil with clouds your glittering
Unholy gaze! . . .
Virgin? . . . You are an aged courtesan
Leering at lovers! . . . leave me, leave me, then!
If you were not half-blind, you'd see
I am alone! . . . Oh, moon . . . stop mocking me!

Trees!
Murmuring to each passing breeze
Ancient mysteries—
Flowers,
Gossiping with drowsy bees
In social, chaste amenities—
Don't you know my heart is breaking?
Can't you sympathize with aching
Human misery?
Are all your little hours
Golden as these?
Or . . . do you hide
Your searching, poignant tragedies,
Under the hard, bright smile of pride?
I think that I shall also go
Laughing, . . . not too loudly . . .
Moving with gracious step and slow,
Quietly . . . proudly . . .
And then, perhaps, no one will know
My heart has died!

Theda Kenyon

The Dandelions

UPON a showery night and still,
Without a sound of warning,

A trooper band surprised the hill,
   And held it in the morning.

We were not waked by bugle-notes,
   No cheer our dreams invaded,
And yet, at dawn, their yellow coats
   On the green slopes paraded.

We careless folk the deed forgot;
   Till one day, idly walking,
We marked upon the self-same spot
   A crowd of veterans talking.

They shook their trembling heads and gray
   With pride and noiseless laughter;
When, well-a-day! they blew away,
   And ne'er were heard of after!

Helen Gray Cone

Rhodora

RHODORA! if the sages ask thee why
   This charm is wasted on the earth and sky,
Tell them, dear, that if eyes were made for seeing
Then Beauty is its own excuse for being:
Why thou wert there, O rival of the rose!
I never thought to ask, I never knew:
But, in my simple ignorance, suppose
The self-same Power that brought me there brought you.

Ralph Waldo Emerson

Daisies

OVER the shoulders and slopes of the dune
 I saw the white daisies go down to the sea,
A host in the sunshine, an army in June,
The people God sends us to set our hearts free.

The bobolinks rallied them up from the dell,
The orioles whistled them out of the wood;
And all of their singing was, "Earth, it is well!"
And all of their dancing was, "Life, thou art good."
Bliss Carman

Out in the Fields with God

THE little cares that fretted me
 I lost them yesterday
Among the fields, above the sea,
 Among the winds at play,
Among the lowing of the herds,
 The rustling of the trees,
Among the singing of the birds,
 The humming of the bees.

The foolish fears of what might happen,
 I cast them all away,
Among the clover-scented grass,
 Among the new mown hay,
Among the husking of the corn,
 Where drowsy poppies nod,
Where ill thoughts die and good are born—
 Out in the fields with God.
Louise Imogen Guiney

The Blackbird

IN the far corner,
  close by the swings,
every morning
a blackbird sings.

His bill's so yellow,
his coat's so black,
that he makes a fellow
whistle back.

Ann, my daughter,
thinks that he
sings for us two
especially.

Humbert Wolfe

The Robin

THE robin is the one
  That interrupts the morn
With hurried, few, express reports
When March is scarcely on.

The robin is the one
That overflows the noon
With her cherubic quantity,
And April but begun.

The robin is the one
That speechless from her nest
Submits that home and certainty
And sanctity are best.

Emily Dickinson.

Clover

LITTLE masters, hat in hand,
Let me in your presence stand,
Till your silence solve for me
This your threefold mystery.

Tell me—for I long to know—
How, in darkness there below,
Was your fairy fabric spun,
Spread and fashioned, three in one.

Did your gossips gold and blue,
Sky and Sunshine, choose for you,
Ere your triple forms were seen,
Suited liveries of green?

Can ye—if ye dwelt indeed
Captives of a prison seed—
Like the Genie, once again
Get you back into the grain?

Little masters, may I stand
In your presence, hat in hand,
Waiting till you solve for me
This your threefold mystery?

John B. Tabb

A Conversation

A LITTLE road goes up the hill,
And Thistle-down says she,
"I'm off a-gipsying today,
Drift up the road with me."

"And sure 'tis nice to go," says I,
"But 'tis not I will come,
For who would feed my cow and cat,
And make my wheel to hum?

'Tis here at home that I will bide,
And thanks to you," says I,
So off went gipsy Thistle-down
A-drifting in the sky.

Sara Hamilton Birchall

A Yellow Pansy

TO the wall of the old green garden
   A butterfly quivering came;
His wings on the sombre lichens
   Played like a yellow flame.

He looked at the gay geraniums,
   And the sleepy four-o'-clocks;
He looked at the low lanes bordered
   With the glossy-growing box.

He longed for the peace and the silence,
   And the shadows that lengthened there,
And his wee wild heart was weary
   Of skimming the endless air.

And now in the old green garden,—
   I know not how it came,—
A single pansy is blooming,
   Bright as a yellow flame.

And whenever a gay gust passes,
  It quivers as if with pain,
For the butterfly-soul that is in it
  Longs for the winds again!

Helen Gray Cone

The Answer

LAVENDER for old loves,
  Roses for the new,
Heliotrope for pleasure, lass,
  And for sorrow, rue.

Rosemary lest you forget.—
  Take, or let it be.
I will have the wholesome pine
  And the open sea.

Rosemary lest you forget.—
  When I come again
Up the old familiar path
  In the autumn rain,

What if you've forgotten, lass?
  Say, what shall I do?—
Here is heartsease by the gate
  With the bitter rue.

Sara Hamilton Birchall

A Prayer

TEACH me, Father, how to go
  Softly as the grasses grow;
Hush my soul to meet the shock

Of the wild world as a rock;
But my spirit, propt with power,
Make as simple as a flower.
Let the dry heart fill its cup,
Like a poppy looking up;
Let life lightly wear her crown,
Like a poppy looking down.

Teach me, Father, how to be
Kind and patient as a tree.
Joyfully the crickets croon
Under shady oak at noon;
Beetle, on his mission bent,
Tarries in that cooling tent.
Let me, also, cheer a spot,
Hidden field or garden grot—
Place where passing souls can rest
On the way and be their best.
Edwin Markham

The Kinship of the Trees

Girl in a Tree

Her legs were long
  And scratched with thistle.
She had a deft,
Enchanting whistle.

Her hands were slim
But strong for lifting
Herself to trees
When winds were shifting.

And there she'd sit
And watch the birds,
And nibble twigs,
And juggle words;

And there she'd lean
And whistle clearly
Till she was God—
Or very nearly.

Frances Frost

Year In, Year Out

YEAR in, year out,
  No matter what the weather—
A blight upon the harvest
Or a storm upon the sea—
Year in, year out,
No matter how the wind blows,
Another ring is added to the evergreen tree.
                                    Kathleen Millay

Twilight of the Wood

LEAF is no more now than corruption's scent,
  But beautiful are the trees above their dead,
This hour with their summer beauties spent,
When desolate of the thousand sweets they shed,
As to that last and western rite made bare,
Their boughs let drop the amber-yielding cup
That leaves no stain upon the crystal air;
And thinly in their midst a tune goes up:
Then who might sing in all the muted wood?
Its waters locked, no single bird, no leaf;
It is not higher than the living blood
Will sound in bodies stony-dull with grief;
And thus, when death has taken all the rest,
Life's self is heard within earth's icy breast.
                                    Léonie Adams

Tree Feelings

I WONDER if they like it—being trees?
I suppose they do. . . .
It must feel good to have the ground so flat,
And feel yourself stand right straight up like that—
So stiff in the middle—and then branch at ease,
Big boughs that arch, small ones that bend and blow,
And all those fringy leaves that flutter so.
You'd think they'd break off at the lower end
When the wind fills them, and their great heads bend.
But then you think of all the roots they drop,
As much at bottom as there is on top,—
A double tree, widespread in earth and air
Like a reflection in the water there.

I guess they like to stand still in the sun
And just breathe out and in, and feel the cool sap run;
And like to feel the rain run through their hair
And slide down to the roots and settle there.
But I think they like the wind best. From the light touch
That lets the leaves whisper and kiss so much,
To the great swinging, tossing, flying wide,
And all the time so stiff and strong inside!
And the big winds, that pull, and make them feel
How long their roots are, and the earth how leal!

And O the blossoms! And the wild seeds lost!
And jewelled martyrdom of fiery frost!
And fruit trees. I'd forgotten. No cold gem,
But to be apples—and bow down with them!

Charlotte Perkins Stetson

ABC'S in Green

THE trees are God's great alphabet:
  With them He writes in shining green
Across the world His thoughts serene.

He scribbles poems against the sky
With a gay, leafy lettering,
For us and for our bettering.

The wind pulls softly at His page,
And every star and bird
Repeats in dutiful delight His word,
And every blade of grass
Flutters to class.

Like a slow child that does not heed,
I stand at summer's knees,
And from the primer of the wood
I spell that life and love are good,
I learn to read.

Leonora Speyer

O Dreamy, Gloomy, Friendly Trees!

O DREAMY, gloomy, friendly trees,
  I came along your narrow track
To bring my gifts unto your knees
  And gifts did you give back;
For when I brought this heart that burns—
  These thoughts that bitterly repine—
And laid them here among the ferns

And the hum of boughs divine,
Ye, vastest breathers of the air,
  Shook down with slow and mighty poise
Your coolness on the human care,
  Your wonder on its toys,
Your greenness on the heart's despair,
  Your darkness on its noise.

Herbert Trench

God, When You Thought of a Pine Tree

GOD, when you thought of a pine tree,
  How did you think of a star?
How did you dream of a damson west,
Crossed by an inky bar?
How did you think of a dear brown pool
Where flocks of shadows are?

God, when you thought of a cobweb,
How did you think of dew?
How did you know a spider's house
Had spangles bright and new?
How did you know we human folk
Would love them as we do?

God, when you patterned a bird's song,
Flung on a silver string,
How did you know the ecstasy
That crystal call would bring?
How did you think of a bubbling throat
And a darling speckled wing?

God, when you chiseled a raindrop,
How did you think of a stem,
Bearing a lovely satin leaf
To hold the tiny gem?
How did you know a million drops
Would deck the morning's hem?

Why did you mate the moonlit night
With honeysuckle vines?
How did you know madeira bloom
Distilled ecstatic wines?
How did you weave the velvet dusk
Where tangled perfumes are?
God, when you thought of a pine tree,
How did you think of a star?

Unknown

The House of the Trees

OPE your doors and take me in,
  Spirit of the wood,
Wash me clean of dust and din,
  Clothe me in your mood.

Take me from the noisy light
  To the sunless peace,
Where at mid-day standeth Night
  Signing Toil's release.

All your dusky twilight stores
  To my senses give;
Take me in and lock the doors,
  Show me how to live.

Lift your leafy roof for me,
  Part your yielding walls:
Let me wander lingeringly
  Through your scented halls.

Ope your doors and take me in,
  Spirit of the wood;
Take me—make me next of kin
  To your leafy brood.
              Ethelwyn Wetherald

Trees

IN the Garden of Eden, planted by God,
There were goodly trees in the springing sod,—

Trees of beauty and height and grace,
To stand in splendor before His face.

Apple and hickory, ash and pear,
Oak and beech and the tulip rare,

The trembling aspen, the noble pine,
The sweeping elm by the river line;

Trees for the birds to build and sing,
And the lilac tree for a joy in spring;

Trees to turn at the frosty call
And carpet the ground for their Lord's footfall;

Trees for fruitage and fire and shade,
Trees for the cunning builder's trade;

Wood for the bow, the spear, and the flail,
The keel and the mast of the daring sail;

He made them of every grain and girth,
For the use of man in the Garden of Earth.

Then lest the soul should not lift her eyes
From the gift to the Giver of Paradise,

On the crown of a hill, for all to see,
God planted a scarlet maple tree.
Bliss Carman

The Trees and the Master

INTO the woods my Master went,
  Clean forspent, forspent.
Into the woods my Master came,
Forspent with love and shame.
But the olives, they were not blind to Him,
The little gray leaves were kind to Him,
The thorn tree had a mind to Him
When into the woods He came.

Out of the woods my Master went,
And He was well content.
Out of the woods my Master came,
Content with death and shame.
When death and shame would woo Him last,
From under the trees they drew Him last,
'Twas on a tree they slew Him—last
When out of the woods He came.
Sidney Lanier

The Trees

THERE'S something in a noble tree—
  What shall I say? a soul?
For 'tis not form, or aught we see
  In leaf or branch or bole.
Some presence, though not understood,
  Dwells there alway, and seems
To be acquainted with our mood,
  And mingles in our dreams.

I would not say that trees at all
  Were of our blood and race,
Yet, lingering where their shadows fall,
  I sometimes think I trace
A kinship, whose far-reaching root
  Grew when the world began,
And made them best of all things mute
  To be the friends of man.

Held down by whatsoever might
  Unto an earthly sod,
They stretch forth arms for air and light,
  As we do after God;
And when in all their boughs the breeze
  Moans loud, or softly sings,
As our own hearts in us, the trees
  Are almost human things.

What wonder in the days that burned
  With old poetic dream,
Dead Phaëthon's fair sisters turned
  To poplars by the stream!
In many a light cotillion stept
  The trees when fluters blew;

And many a tear, 'tis said, they wept
  For human sorrow too.

Mute, said I? They are seldom thus;
  They whisper each to each,
And each and all of them to us,
  In varied forms of speech.
"Be serious," the solemn pine
  Is saying overhead;
"Be beautiful," the elm-tree fine
  Has always finely said;

"Be quick to feel," the aspen still
  Repeats the whole day long;
While, from the green slope of the hill,
  The oak-tree adds, "Be strong."
When with my burden, as I hear
  Their distant voices call,
I rise, and listen, and draw near,
  "Be patient," say they all.
               Samuel Valentine Cole

Three Trees

THE poplar is a French tree,
  A tall and laughing wench tree,
A slender tree, a tender tree,
That whispers to the rain—
An easy, breezy flapper tree,
A lithe and blithe and dapper tree,
A girl of trees, a pearl of trees,
Beside the shallow Aisne.

The oak is a British tree,
And not at all a skittish tree;
A rough tree, a tough tree,
A knotty tree to bruise;
A drives-his-roots-in-deep tree,
A mighty tree, a blighty tree,
A tree of stubborn thews.

The pine tree is our own tree,
A grown tree, a cone tree,
The tree to face a bitter wind,
The tree for mast and spar—
A mounting tree, a fine tree,
A fragrant turpentine tree,
A limber tree, a timber tree,
And resinous with tar!

Christopher Morley

What do we Plant

WHAT do we plant when we plant the tree?
We plant the ship which will cross the sea.
We plant the mast to carry the sails;
We plant the planks to withstand the gales—
The keel, the keelson, and beam and knee;
We plant the ship when we plant the tree.

What do we plant when we plant the tree?
We plant the houses for you and me.
We plant the rafters, the shingles, the floors,
We plant the studding, the lath, the doors,
The beams and siding, all parts that be;
We plant the house when we plant the tree.

What do we plant when we plant the tree?
A thousand things that we daily see;
We plant the spire that out-towers the crag,
We plant the staff for our country's flag,
We plant the shade, from the hot sun free;
We plant all these when we plant the tree!
Henry Abbey

Trees

MANY a tree is found in the wood,
And every tree for its use is good.
Some for the strength of the gnarlèd root,
Some for the sweetness of flower or fruit,
Some for shelter against the storm,
And some to keep the hearthstone warm,
Some for the roof and some for the beam,
And some for a boat to breast the storm.
In the wealth of the wood since the world began,
The trees have offered their gifts to man.

But the glory of trees is more than their gifts:
'Tis a beautiful wonder of life that lifts
From a wrinkled seed in an earth-bound clod
A column, an arch in the temple of God,
A pillar of power, a dome of delight,
A shrine of song and a joy of sight!
Their roots are the nurses of rivers in birth,
Their leaves are alive with the breath of the earth;
They shelter the dwellings of man, and they bend
O'er his grave with the look of a loving friend.

I have camped in the whispering forest of pines
I have slept in the shadow of olives and vines;
In the knees of an oak, at the foot of a palm,
I have found good rest and slumber's balm.
And now, when the morning gilds the boughs
Of the vaulted elm at the door of my house,
I open the window and make a salute:
"God bless thy branches and feed thy root!
Thou hast lived before, live after me,
Thou ancient, friendly, faithful tree!"

Henry van Dyke

The Trees

TIME is never wasted listening to the trees;
  If to heaven so grandly we arose as these,
Holding toward each other half their kindly grace,
Haply we were worthier of our human place.

Bending down to meet you on the hillside path,
Birch and oak and maple each his welcome hath;
Each his own fine cadence, his familiar word,
By the ear accustomed, always plainly heard.

Every tree gives answer to some different mood,
This one helps you climbing; that for rest is good;
Beckoning friends, companions, sentinels they are;
Good to live and die with, good to greet afar.

Lucy Larcom

Good Company

TO-DAY I have grown taller from walking with the trees,
The seven sister-poplars who go softly in a line;

And I think my heart is whiter for its parley with a star
That trembled out at nightfall and hung above the pine.

The call-note of a redbird from the cedars in the dusk
Woke his happy mate within me to an answer free and fine;
And a sudden angel beckoned from a column of blue smoke—
Lord, who am I that they should stoop—these holy folk of thine?

Karle Wilson Baker

The Green Tree In The Fall

DID you forget to bud in Spring,
O Green Tree in the Fall,
That now you wear these fresh young leaves
As for a coronal?

All of your mates within the wood
Are in the crimson leaf,
They had their swift, enamored spring,
Their summertime too brief.

But you—what chance befell that you
Were cheated of the Spring,
That now you cling so fast to leaves
Wherein no bird will sing?

My heart is with you, little tree,
For I was cheated too,
And now I grasp at what I missed
And cling as fast as you.

Jessie B. Rittenhouse

The Call of the Sea

Bag-Pipes at Sea

ABOVE the shouting of the gale,
   The whipping sheet, the dashing spray,
I heard, with notes of joy and wail,
   A piper play.

Along the dipping deck he trod,
   The dusk about his shadowy form;
He seemed like some strange ancient god
   Of song and storm.

He gave his dim-seen pipes a skirl
   And war went down the darkling air;
Then came a sudden subtle swirl,
   And love was there.

What were the winds that flailed and flayed
   The sea to him, the night obscure?
In dreams he strayed some brackened glade,
   Some heathery moor.

And if he saw the slanting spars,
   And if he watched the shifting track,
He marked, too, the eternal stars
   Shine through the wrack.

And so amid the deep sea din,
   And so amid the wastes of foam,
Afar his heart was happy in
   His highland home!

Clinton Scollard

Young Sea

THE sea is never still.
   It pounds on the shore
Restless as a young heart,
Hunting.

The sea speaks
And only the stormy hearts
Know what it says:
It is the face
      of a rough mother speaking.

The sea is young.
One storm cleans all the hoar
And loosens the age of it.
I hear it laughing, reckless.

They love the sea,
Men who ride on it
And know they will die
Under the salt of it.

Let only the young come,
   Says the sea.
Let them kiss my face
   And hear me.
I am the last word
   And I tell
Where storms and stars come from.

Carl Sandburg

Sea-Fever

I MUST down to the seas again, to the lonely sea and the sky,
And all I ask is a tall ship and a star to steer her by,
And the wheel's kick and the wind's song and the white sail's shaking,
And a gray mist on the sea's face and a gray dawn breaking.

I must down to the seas again, for the call of the running tide
Is a wild call and a clear call that may not be denied;
And all I ask is a windy day with the white clouds flying,
And the flung spray and the blown spume, and the sea-gulls crying.

I must down to the seas again to the vagrant gypsy life,
To the gull's way and the whale's way where the wind's like a whetted knife;
And all I ask is a merry yarn from a laughing fellow-rover,
And quiet sleep and a sweet dream when the long trick's over.

John Masefield

A Son of the Sea

I WAS born for deep-sea faring;
I was bred to put to sea;
Stories of my father's daring
Filled me at my mother's knee.

I was sired among the surges;
I was cubbed beside the foam;
All my heart is in its verges,
And the sea wind is my home.

All my boyhood, from far vernal
Bournes of being, came to me
Dream-like, plangent, and eternal
Memories of the plunging sea.

Bliss Carman

Dreams of the Sea

I KNOW not why I yearn for thee again,
   To sail once more upon thy fickle flood;
I'll hear thy waves wash under my death-bed,
   Thy salt is lodged forever in my blood.

Yet I have seen thee lash the vessel's sides
   In fury, with thy many tailèd whip;
And I have seen thee, too, like Galilee,
   When Jesus walked in peace to Simon's ship.

And I have seen thy gentle breeze as soft
   As summer's, when it makes the cornfields run;
And I have seen thy rude and lusty gale
   Make ships show half their bellies to the sun.

Thou knowest the way to tame the wildest life,
   Thou knowest the way to bend the great and proud:
I think of that Armada whose puffed sails,
   Greedy and large, came swallowing every cloud.

But I have seen the sea-boy, young and drowned
  Lying on shore and, by thy cruel hand,
A seaweed beard was on his tender chin,
  His heaven-blue eyes were filled with common sand.

And yet, for all, I yearn for thee again,
  To sail once more upon thy fickle flood:
I'll hear thy waves wash under my death-bed,
  Thy salt is lodged forever in my blood.
William H. Davies

Going Down in Ships

GOING down to sea in ships
  Is a glorious thing,
Where up and over the rolling waves
  The sea-birds wing;

Oh, there's nothing more to my heart's desire
  Than a ship that plows
Head-on down through marching seas,
  With streaming bows:

Would you hear the song of the viewless winds
  As they walk the sky?
Come down to sea when the storm is on
  And the men stand by.

Would you see the sun as it walked abroad
  On God's First Day?
Then come where dawn makes sea and sky
  A gold causeway.

Oh, it's bend the sails on the criss-cross yards,
  For the day dies far,
And up a windless space of dusk
  Climbs the evening star. . . .

Now there's gulf on foaming gulf of stars
  That lean so clear
That it seems the bastions of heaven
  Are bright and near,

And that, any moment, the topmost sky
  May froth and swim
With an incredible bivouac
  Of seraphim. . . .

O wide-flung dawn, O mighty day
  And set of sun!
O all you climbing stars of God,
  Oh, lead me on! . . .

Harry Kemp

The Waves of Breffny

THE grand road from the mountain goes shining to
    the sea,
  And there is traffic in it and many a horse and cart,
But the little roads of Cloonagh are dearer far to me,
  And the little roads of Cloonagh go rambling through
    my heart.

A great storm from the ocean goes shouting o'er the hill,
  And there is glory in it; and terror on the wind:
But the haunted air of twilight is very strange and still,
  And the little winds of twilight are dearer to my mind.

The great waves of the Atlantic sweep storming on their way,
  Shining green and silver with the hidden herring shoal;
But the little waves of Breffny have drenched my heart in spray,
  And the little waves of Breffny go stumbling through my soul.

Eva Gore-Booth

Short Beach

OH, the salt wind in my nostrils!
  And the white sail in the creek!
And the blue beyond the marshes!
  And the flag at the peak!

My soul lifts to the bugles
  Of a far cry on the breeze—
The cry of my storm-kin calling
  Overseas, overseas!

Blow, horns of the old sea-rapture!
  When your call comes from afar,
I would rise from the grave to reach you
  Where the sea-dooms are.

Richard Hovey

Sea Call

MY old love for the water has come back again—
  I had forgotten its surging, so long, so long away;
Sapphire-blue in the sunlight and green-gray in the rain,

And the same waves cresting, and the same sharp spray,
There was left a wave in my heart when I went to the in-
    land towns,
  Something that moved and murmured in the days when
    I forgot;
Vivid flowers of the gardens or thick long grass of the
    downs—
  What were the sweets of the summer days, where the
    calling waves were not?

My old love for the water has come back once more;
  The wave of the deep draws full, and the wave in my
    heart lifts high;
This is my own old country and my own old shore . . .
  And I cannot leave the water till the day I die.
                                        Margaret Widdemer

Ship-Love

WHEN God gave to all men
    All the earth to love
He gave them the waters under the sea,
He gave them the sky above;
And some love the waters,
And some love the sky;
But I love the tall ships
That go sailing by.

For when God gave to my heart
The warm living blood
He gave me, too, the passion
For ebb-tide and flood;
And my love is ship-love,

For tall ships and strange,
For steam-ships and sailing ships
The whole wide range.

And when God calls my spirit
And claims the soul of me
He'll find it a-wandering
With ships on the sea;
He'll find it on a warm deck
Dreaming in the sun,
Long after I am perished
And my earth-life done.

Ethel E. Mannin

The Sea

I CALL thee from the changing land
To the unchanging sea;
I bring a bride-gift in my hand
Of immortality.
The land is fair, but fairer far
The pastures of the sea.
Canst thou reach down the lowest star?
My sea-fires gleam for thee.
All rivers run unto one end
And perish in the sea;
Turn thou from lover and from friend,
And give thy heart to me.
Thy love shall suffer change and dearth,
Thy friend the years estrange;
There is no faithfulness on earth—
The sea will never change.

Nora Hopper

Coquette

I AM wearied with insatiable longing
  For that laughing, blue-eyed wanton called the sea.
 Though she's but a faithless rover
 And the wide world's willing lover
I'd be content if she would share an hour with me.

 If she would toss me on her restless, throbbing bosom,
Caress a moment—and then flout me in my pain,
 I would barter all the treasures
 Of the rich man's million pleasures
To be rocked within her siren arms again.

 Her honey voice is luring, mocking, calling!
Her sapphire scalloped skirts are piped with foam:
 And her light feet shoreward dancing,
 Pearly-sandalled and entrancing,
Entice the steps of men from love and home.

 False and cruel is her glittering lure;
Her gifts are death and woe's delirium—
 Yet heaven holds no blisses
 Like the sharp tang of her kisses—
Ah! Coquette! if you should slay me, I must come!

Keith Stuart

The Deep Water Man

O GIVE me the Pole Star overhead,
  A slithering deck to my feet,
A forward bunk for my downy bed,

And the sea for my village street,
The galley's glow for my warm hearthstone,
And my mates for my kin and friends—
Then earth's long leagues are my very own
To the place where the round world ends.

There's never a richer man than I,
Nor a poorer under the sun;
For all of my boundless riches lie
In the things I have seen and done—
The songs I've sung and the laughs I've laughed—
Oh, that's wealth as it ought to be,
For when the Skipper shall call me aft
I can take it along with me.

A-roaring down the Atlantic lanes,
Or cruising a tropical sea,
The balmy Trades, or the wind-whipped rains,
Are a bit of the same to me.
I'm home wherever the anchors fall
And take my idolatrous ease—
I've got a girl in each port of call
To be found on the seven seas.

Oh, loves I've known that were deep and strong,
Of some ports I am more than fond,
But woman nor town can hold me long
From the call of the ones beyond.
So, ever and always outward bound
(Well, I guess it's the fate of some)
Till the day their keels go hard aground
In the Port of the Kingdom Come.
James Stuart Montgomery

Sea Longing

YOU who are inland born know not the pain
  Of one who longs for gray dunes and the seas
And sound of ebbing tide and windy rain
And sea-mews crying down immensities.
You who are inland born, know not the urge
Of rapt tides beating passionate and wild;
Nor have you thrilled with wonder at the surge
Of drifting water, wayward as a child.
Impetuous I seek the eager sea,
Imperious for joy and wind-blown spray;
You, who are city-beaten every day,
What do you know of mirth and ecstasy?
No thirsty wind has journeyed from the South—
And laid a cool, wet finger on your mouth!

Harold Vinal

Had I the Choice

HAD I the choice to tally greatest bards,
  To limn their portraits, stately, beautiful, and emulate at will,
Homer with all his wars and warriors—Hector, Achilles, Ajax,
Or Shakspere's woe-entangled Hamlet, Lear, Othello—
   Tennyson's fair ladies,
Metre or wit the best, or choice conceit to wield in perfect
   rhyme, delight of singers;
These, these, O sea, all these I'd gladly barter,
Would you the undulation of one wave, its trick to me
   transfer,
Or breathe one breath of yours upon my verse,
  And leave its odor there.

Walt Whitman

Gray

A BLEAK wind is riding on the waves,
  And the shadowy foam is hurled;
And the gray rains are on the hills
  And a gray dusk is over the world.

And bleak moods and shadowy moods
  Move like the moods of the sea,
And mist, like a gray unspoken thought,
  Is looking strangely at me.

And I am lost in grayness,
  My dreams are still and furled,
For the gray rains are on the hills
  And a gray dusk is over the world.
                    Oscar Williams

A Pagan Hymn

I HAVE drunk the Sea's good wine,
  And to-day
Care has bowed his head and gone away.
I have drunk the Sea's good wine,
Was ever step so light as mine,
Was ever heart so gay?
Old voices intermingle in my brain,
Voices that a little boy might hear,
And dreams like fiery sunsets come again,
Informulate and vain,
But great with glories of the buccaneer.
Oh, thanks to thee, great Mother, thanks to thee,
For this old joy renewed,

For tightened sinew and clear blood imbued
With sunlight and with sea.
Behold, I sing a pagan song of old,
And out of my full heart,
Hold forth my hands that so I would enfold
The Infinite thou art.
What matter all the creeds that come and go,
The many gods of men?
My blood outcasts them from its joyous flow,
And it is now as then—
The Pearl of Morning, and the Sapphire Sea,
The Diamond of Noon,
The Ruby of the Sunset—these shall be
My creed, my Deity;
And I will take some old forgotten tune,
And rhythm frolic-free,
And sing in little words thy wondrous boon,
O Sunlight and O Sea!

John Runcie

As the Tide Comes In

THE long-winged terns dart wild and dire,
  As the tide comes tumbling in.
The calm rock-pools grow all alive,
With the tide tumbling in,
The crab that under the brown weed creeps,
And the snail who lies in his house and sleeps,
Awake and stir, as the plunging sweep
Of the tide comes tumbling in.

The driftwood swishes along the sand,
As the tide comes tumbling in.

With wreck and wrack from many a land,
On the tide, tumbling in.
About my feet are a broken spar,
A pale anemone's torn sea-star
And scattered scum of the waves' old war,
As the tide comes tumbling in.

And, oh, there is a stir at the heart of me,
As the tide comes tumbling in.
All life once more is a part of me,
As the tide tumbles in.
New hopes awaken beneath despair
And thoughts slip free of the sloth of care,
While beauty and love are everywhere—
As the tide comes tumbling in.

Cale Young Rice

A Wet Sheet and a Flowing Sea

A WET sheet and a flowing sea,—
  A wind that follows fast,
That fills the white and rustling sail,
  And bends the gallant mast,—
And bends the gallant mast, my boys,
  While, like the eagle free,
Away the good ship flies, and leaves
  Old England on the lee.

Oh, for a soft and gentle wind!
  I heard a fair one cry;
But give to me the snoring breeze,
  And white waves heaving high,—

And white waves heaving high, my boys,
   The good ship tight and free;
The world of waters is our home,
   And merry men are we.

There's tempest in yon hornèd moon,
   And lightning in yon cloud;
And hark the music, mariners!
   The wind is piping loud,—
The wind is piping loud, my boys,
   The lightning flashing free;
While the hollow oak our palace is,
   Our heritage the sea.

Allan Cunningham

The Undersong

I HEAR the sea-song of the blood in my heart,
I hear the sea-song of the blood in my ears:
And I am far apart,
And lost in the years.

But when I lie and dream of that which was
Before the first man's shadow flitted on the grass,
I am stricken dumb
With sense of that to come.

Is then this wildering sea-song but a part
Of the old song of the mystery of the years—
Or only the echo of the tirèd heart
And of tears?

Fiona Macleod

Gray Rocks and Grayer Sea

GRAY rocks, and grayer sea,
  And surf along the shore—
And in my heart a name
  My lips shall speak no more.

The high and lonely hills
  Endure the darkening year—
And in my heart endure
  A memory and a tear.

Across the tide a sail
  That tosses, and is gone—
And in my heart the kiss
  That longing dreams upon.

Gray rocks, and grayer sea,
  And surf along the shore—
And in my heart the face
  That I shall see no more.

Charles G. D. Roberts

The Sea

THE Sea! the Sea! the open Sea!
  The blue, the fresh, the ever free!
Without a mark, without a bound,
It runneth the earth's wide regions round;
It plays with the clouds; it mocks the skies;
Or like a cradled creature lies.

I'm on the Sea! I'm on the Sea!
I am where I would ever be;
With the blue above, and the blue below,
And silence wheresoe'er I go;
If a storm should come and awake the deep,
What matter? I shall ride and sleep.

I love (oh! how I love) to ride
On the fierce foaming bursting tide,
When every mad wave drowns the moon,
Or whistles aloft his tempest tune,
And tells how goeth the world below,
And why the south-west blasts do blow.

I never was on the dull tame shore,
But I lov'd the great Sea more and more,
And backward flew to her billowy breast,
Like a bird that seeketh its mother's nest;
And a mother she was, and is to me;
For I was born on the open Sea.

The waves were white, and red the morn,
In the noisy hour when I was born;
And the whale it whistled, the porpoise rolled,
And the dolphins bared their backs of gold;
And never was heard such an outcry wild
As welcomed to life the Ocean-child!

I've lived since then, in calm and strife,
Full fifty summers a sailor's life,
With wealth to spend and a power to range,
But never have sought, nor sighed for change;
And Death, whenever he come to me,
Shall come on the wide unbounded Sea!

Bryan Waller Procter

The Sea Road

OH, green curved the hill road and beckoned to my feet,
  Where the breath of the uplands came drifting fitful-sweet.
Moon mist, and cloud mist, and meadows drenched with dew,
Fir breath, and fern breath, and hill-winds stealing through
To stir the vagrant poppy-blooms that gipsy through the wheat.

  But nearer and clearer than these there called to me
  A little, waiting, dune-set road that comrades with the sea.

Oh, bright shone the plains' road in ribbonings of gold,
Past lowly cottage casements tucked beneath a green hill's fold.
Peat smoke, and hearth smoke, and toiler's wayside fire,
Wife love, and child's love, and humble hearts' desire,
Peace and fireside plenty was the tale its windings told.

  Yet nearer and clearer than these there called to me
  A small road, dark with juniper, and open to the sea.

A little, watchful, sea-wife road unmindful of the gales,
All kirtled blue with sunlit waves, and coiffed with speeding sails.
Far sail, and near sail, the beating sea-gulls' wings,
Far lands, the near lands, the lullaby she sings,
All the ports of all the world are in her whispered tales.

  Ah, nearer and dearer than all there cries to me,
  One little, crooning, sunset road set shoulder to the sea.
  Martha Haskell Clarke

The Sea[1]

I

INTERMINABLE, not to be divined,
  The ocean's solemn distances recede;
A gospel of glad color to the mind,
  But for the soul a voice of sterner creed.
The sadness of unfathomable things
  Calls from the waste and makes the heart give heed
With answering dirges, as a seashell sings.

II

Mother of infinite loss! Mother bereft!
  Thou of the shaken hair! Far-questing Sea!
Sea of the lapsing wail of waves! O left
  Of many lovers! Lone, lamenting Sea!
Desolate, prone, disheveled, lost, sublime!
  Unquelled and reckless! Mad, despairing Sea!
Wail, for I wait—wail, ancient dirge of Time!

III

Stretch wide, O marshes, in your golden joy!
  Stretch ample, marshes, in serene delight!
Proclaiming faith past tempest to destroy,
  With silent confidence of conscious might!
Glad of the blue sky, knowing nor wind nor rain
  Can do your large indifference despite,
Nor lightning mar your tolerant disdain!

[1] Extracts from "Seaward," an Elegy.

IV

The fanfare of the trumpets of the sea
   Assaults the air with jubilant foray;
The intolerable exigence of glee
   Shouts to the sun and leaps in radiant spray;
The laughter of the breakers on the shore
   Shakes like the mirth of Titans heard at play,
With thunders of tumultuous uproar.

V

Playmate of terrors! Intimate of Doom!
   Fellow of Fate and Death! Exultant Sea!
Thou strong companion of the Sun, make room!
   Let me make one with you, rough comrade Sea!
Sea of the boisterous sport of wind and spray!
   Sea of the lion mirth! Sonorous Sea!
I hear thy shout, I know what thou wouldst say.

VI

Dauntless, triumphant, reckless of alarms,
   O Queen that laughest Time and Fear to scorn,
Death, like a bridegroom, tosses in thine arms.
   The rapture of your fellowship is borne
Like music on the wind. I hear the blare,
   The calling of the undesisting horn,
And tremors as of trumpets on the air.

Richard Hovey

The World is Too Much With Us

THE World is too much with us; late and soon,
   Getting and spending, we lay waste our powers;
Little we see in Nature that is ours;
We have given our hearts away, a sordid boon!

This Sea that bares her bosom to the moon,
The winds that will be howling at all hours
And are up-gather'd now like sleeping flowers,
For this, for every thing, we are out of tune;

It moves us not.—Great God! I'd rather be
A Pagan suckled in a creed outworn,—
So might I, standing on this pleasant lea,
Have glimpses that would make me less forlorn;
Have sight of Proteus rising from the sea;
Or hear old Triton blow his wreathèd horn.
                      William Wordsworth

Sunrise

DAY!
   Faster and more fast,
O'er night's brim, day boils at last:
Boils, pure gold, o'er the cloud-cup's brim
Where spurting and suppressed it lay,
For not a froth-flake touched the rim
Of yonder gap in the solid gray
Of the eastern cloud, an hour away;
But forth one wavelet, then another, curled,

Till the whole sunrise, not to be suppressed,
Rose, reddened, and its seething breast
Flickered in bounds, grew gold, then overflowed the world.
                                        Robert Browning

Song of the Sea

THE song of the sea was an ancient song
   In the days when the earth was young;
The waves were gossiping loud and long
Ere mortals had found a tongue;
The heart of the waves with wrath was wrung
Or soothed to a siren strain,
As they tossed the primitive isles among
Or slept in the open main.
Such was the song and its changes free,
   Such was the song of the sea.

The song of the sea took a human tone
In the days of the coming of man;
A mournfuller meaning swelled her moan,
And fiercer her riots ran;
Because that her stately voice began
To speak of our human woes;
With music mighty to grasp and span
Life's tale and its passion-throes.
Such was the song as it grew to be,
   Such was the song of the sea.

The song of the sea was a hungry sound
As the human years unrolled;
For the notes were hoarse with the doomed **and drowned**,
Or choked with a shipwreck's gold;

Till it seemed no dirge above the mould
So sorry a story said
As the midnight cry of the waters old
Calling above their dead.
Such is the song and its threnody,
   Such is the song of the sea.

The song of the sea is a wondrous lay,
For it mirrors human life;
It is grave and great as the judgment day,
It is torn with the thought of strife;
Yet under the stars it is smooth and rife
With love-lights everywhere,
When the sky has taken the deep to wife
And their wedding-day is fair—
Such is the ocean's mystery,
   Such is the song of the sea.

Richard Burton

Farewell

NOT soon shall I forget—a sheet
   Of golden water, cold and sweet,
The young moon with her head in veils
Of silver, and the nightingales.

A wain of hay came up the lane—
O fields I shall not walk again,
And trees I shall not see, so still
Against a sky of daffodil!

Fields where my happy heart had rest,
And where my heart was heaviest,

I shall remember them at peace
Drenched in moon-silver like a fleece.

The golden water sweet and cold,
The moon of silver and of gold,
The dew upon the gray grass-spears,
I shall remember them with tears.
Katherine Tynan

The Return [1]

I WILL go back to the great sweet mother,
Mother and lover of men, the sea.
I will go down to her, I and none other,
   Close with her, kiss her, and mix her with me;
Cling to her, strive with her, hold her fast;
O fair white mother, in days long past
Born without sister, born without brother,
   Set free my soul as thy soul is free.

O fair green-girdled mother of mine,
   Sea, that art clothed with the sun and the rain,
Thy sweet hard kisses are strong like wine,
   Thy large embraces are keen like pain.
Save me and hide me with all thy waves,
Find me one grave of thy thousand graves,
Those pure cold populous graves of thine,
   Wrought without hand in a world without stain.

I shall sleep, and move with the moving ships,
   Change as the winds change, veer in the tide;
My lips will feast on the foam of thy lips,

I shall rise with thy rising, with thee subside;
Sleep, and not know if she be, if she were,
Filled full with life to the eyes and hair,
As a rose is fulfilled to the roseleaf tips
    With splendid summer and perfume and pride.

This woven raiment of nights and days,
    Were it once cast off and unwound from me,
Naked and glad would I walk in thy ways,
    Alive and aware of thy ways and thee;
Clear of the whole world, hidden at home,
Clothed with the green and crowned with the foam,
A pulse of the life of thy straits and bays,
    A vein in the heart of the streams of the sea.

Fair mother, fed with the lives of men,
    Thou art subtle and cruel of heart, men say
Thou hast taken, and shalt not render again;
    Thou art full of thy dead, and cold as they.
But death is the worst that comes of thee;
Thou art fed with our dead, O mother, O sea,
But when hast thou fed on our hearts? or when,
    Having given us love, hast thou taken away?

O tender-hearted, O perfect lover,
    Thy lips are bitter, and sweet thine heart.
Thy hopes that hurt and the dreams that hover,
    Shall they not vanish away and apart?
But thou, thou art sure, thou art older than earth;
Thou art strong for death and fruitful of birth;
Thy depths conceal and thy gulfs discover;
    From the first thou wert, from the end thou art.
Algernon Charles Swinburne

The Port O' Heart's Desire

DOWN around the quay they lie, the ships that sail to sea,
On shore the brown-cheeked sailormen they pass the jest with me,
But soon their ships will sail away with winds that never tire,
And there's one that will be sailing to the Port o' Heart's Desire.

The Port o' Heart's Desire, and it's, oh, that port for me,
And that's the ship that I love best of all that sail the sea;
Its hold is filled with memories, its prow it points away
To the Port o' Heart's Desire, where I roamed a boy at play.

Ships that sail for gold there be, and ships that sail for fame,
And some were filled with jewels bright when from Cathay they came,
But give me still yon white sail in the sunset's mystic fire,
That the running tides will carry to the Port o' Heart's Desire.

It's you may have the gold and fame, and all the jewels, too,
And all the ships, if they were mine, I'd gladly give to you,
I'd give them all right gladly, with their gold and fame entire,
If you would set me down within the Port o' Heart's Desire.

Oh, speed you, white-winged ship of mine, oh, speed you to the sea,
Some other day, some other tide, come back again for me;

Come back with all the memories, the joys and e'en the pain,
And take me to the golden hills of boyhood once again.
John S. McGroarty

Sea Urge

OH, to feel the tremble of a ship beneath my feet again,
Now that April's urge is running riot in the tide,
Where gray gull dips to white gull and the salt spray leaps to meet them
Out across blue water where the tall ships ride.

Freshets in the mountain streams and floods along the river
Go rushing down to join the tossing tumult of the sea.
And the April urge that drives them sets the sailor's heart aquiver
With the joy of ocean madness when the sails flap free.
Unknown

The Ocean

THERE is a pleasure in the pathless woods,
There is a rapture on the lonely shore,
There is society, where none intrudes,
By the deep Sea, and music in its roar:
I love not man the less, but Nature more,
From these our interviews, in which I steal
From all I may be, or have been before,
To mingle with the Universe, and feel
What I can ne'er express, yet cannot all conceal.

Roll on, thou deep and dark blue ocean—roll!
Ten thousand fleets sweep over thee in vain;
Man marks the earth with ruin—his control
Stops with the shore;—upon the watery plain
The wrecks are all thy deed, nor doth remain
A shadow of man's ravage, save his own,
When, for a moment, like a drop of rain,
He sinks into thy depth with bubbling groan,
Without a grave, unknelled, uncoffined, and unknown.

His steps are not upon thy paths,—thy fields
Are not a spoil for him,—thou dost arise
And shake him from thee; the vile strength he wields
For earth's destruction thou dost all despise,
Spurning him from thy bosom to the skies,
And send'st him, shivering in thy playful spray,
And howling, to his Gods, where haply lies
His petty hope in some near port or bay,
And dashest him again to earth:—there let him lay.

. . . .

Thou glorious mirror, where the Almighty's form
Glasses itself in tempests; in all time,
Calm or convulsed—in breeze, or gale, or storm,
Icing the pole, or in the torrid clime
Dark-heaving;—boundless, endless, and sublime—
The image of Eternity—the throne
Of the Invisible; even from out thy slime
The monsters of the deep are made; each zone
Obeys thee; thou goest forth, dread, fathomless, alone.

And I have loved thee, Ocean! and my joy
Of youthful sports was on thy breast to be
Borne, like thy bubbles, onward: from a boy
I wantoned with thy breakers—they to me
Were a delight; and if the freshening sea

Made them a terror—'twas a pleasing fear,
For I was, as it were, a child of thee,
And trusted to thy billows far and near,
And laid my hand upon thy mane—as I do here.
Lord Byron

A Song of Desire

THOU dreamer with the million moods,
   Of restless heart like me,
Lay thy white hands against my breast
   And cool its pain, O Sea!

O wanderer of the unseen paths,
   Restless of heart as I,
Blow hither, from thy caves of blue,
   Wind of the healing sky!

O treader of the fiery way,
   With passionate heart like mine,
Hold to my lips thy healthful cup
   Brimmed with its blood-red wine!

O countless watchers of the night,
   Of sleepless heart like me,
Pour your white beauty in my soul,
   Till I grow calm as ye!

O Sea, O Sun, O Wind and Stars,
   (O hungry heart that longs!)
Feed my starved lips with life, with love,
   And touch my tongue with songs!
Frederic Lawrence Knowles

A Sea Change

HEAVY with unshed tears—weary with pain,
  At last life brought me to the sea again,
Where beauty spoke above my grief's demands.
I heard the singing surf—watched sea-birds fly;
I saw a pine-tree etched against the sky,
And crushed the bay-leaves in my tired hands.

Loveliness filled my spirit like a cup:
A sense of healing and of peace welled up
Which but the sea to the sea-lover brings.
I did not hope; I did not even pray;
But as upon that sun-warmed rock I lay
Joy stirred within me with a lift of wings.
Dorothy Peace

Twilight At Sea

THE twilight hours, like birds, flew by,
  As lightly and as free,
Ten thousand stars were in the sky,
  Ten thousand on the sea;
For every wave, with dimpled face,
  That leaped upon the air,
Had caught a star in its embrace,
  And held it trembling there.
Amelia C. Welby

Sea-Song

TO-DAY was a sea-gull day, dear heart, to-day was a sea-gull day,
With a touch of wind, and the beat of surf, and the breath of the driven spray
Blue of the sky, and blue of the sea, and the white clouds scudding far,
And my longings swept to the sky-line dim like moths to a candle star.

To-day was a sea-gull day, dear heart, that sparkled with sun-flecked blue,
But it bound my heart with a wave-linked chain and bore it away from you.
It stole it far from my hearth and you, though we two sat side by side,
For my heart it tugged like an anchored ship that strains with the seaward tide.

And when we wandered back home, dear heart, so soberly wandered home,
My eyes were blind with the sun-washed gold, and dim with the lunging foam,
And my heart came swaggering on beside, from the wake of the distant ships,
With the lilt of a deep sea chanty-strain like wine on its reckless lips!

Martha Haskell Clark

Deep Down

THE lights are on the harbor,
  And the ships at anchor ride—
Blow she high, blow she low, let 'er blow!

We're outward bound at dawning
With the turning of the tide,
And Davy Jones is waiting down below,
Old Davy Jones is watching down below, below, below,
Down deep, deep down, down below.

Now, here's to hearty weather,
And here's to starry skies—
Up she goes, down she goes, bullies, Oh!
And here's to all the ladies,
And damn old Davy's eyes,
Long may we keep him waiting down below!
Old thieving, crimping Davy, down below, below, below,
Down deep, deep down, down below.

At Rio, Hull or Sidney,
I'll meet you all again,
So here's good luck, my bullies, ere we go,
Or I'll find a berth 'longside you
In the port o' missing men,
Where Davy Jones is waiting down below,
Where Davy Jones is watching down below, below, below,
Down deep, deep down, down below.
                                James Stuart Montgomery

Flood Tide

SHE was born inland in the open country.
She had lived inland and had never seen the sea.
Hence, her only notion
Of the rhythm of the ocean
Was the flowing of a wheatfield or a windswept lea.

Now she holds a letter with "regret to inform you—"
And the sea comes lashing inland with its sullen tongue.
Now the sodden ocean
Holds the lad of her devotion.
Now her eyes are wet with seafoam, and her heart, salt stung.
Marjorie Alice Miller

The Winds of Heaven

South Wind

WHERE have you been, South Wind, this May-day morning?
With larks aloft, or skimming with the swallow,
Or with blackbirds in a green, sun-glinted thicket?

O, I heard you like a tyrant in the valley;
Your ruffian haste shook the young blossoming orchards;
You clapped rude hands, hallooing round the chimney,
And white your pennons streamed along the river.

You have robbed the bee, South Wind, in your adventure,
Blustering with gentle flowers; but I forgave you
When you stole to me shyly with scent of hawthorn.

Siegfried Sassoon

The Roaring Frost

A FLOCK of winds came winging from the North,
Strong birds with fighting pinions driving forth
With a resounding call!

Where will they close their wings and cease their cries—
Between what warming seas and conquering skies—
And fold, and fall?

Alice Meynell

Cook County

THE northeast wind was the wind off the lake
  Blowing the oak-leaves pale side out like
Aspen: blowing the sound of the surf far
Inland over the fences: blowing for
Miles over smell of the earth the lake smell in.

The southwest wind was thunder in afternoon.
You saw the wind first in the trumpet vine
And the green went white with the sky and the weather-vane
Whirled on the barn and the doors slammed altogether.
After the rain in the grass we used to gather
Wind-fallen cold white apples.

                    The west
Wind was the August wind, the wind over waste
Valleys over the waterless plains where still
Were skulls of the buffalo, where in the sand stale
Dung lay of wild cattle. The west wind blew
Day after day as the winds on the plains blow
Burning the grass, turning the leaves brown, filling
Noon with the bronze of cicadas, far out falling
Dark on the colorless water, the lake where not
Waves were nor movement.

                    The north wind was at night
When no leaves and the husk on the oak stirs
Only nor birds then. The north wind was stars
Over the whole sky and snow in the ways
And snow on the sand where in summer the water was. . . .
                              Archibald MacLeish

Do You Fear the Wind?

DO you fear the force of the wind,
   The slash of the rain?
Go face them and fight them,
Be savage again.
Go hungry and cold like the wolf,
Go wade like the crane:
The palms of your hands will thicken,
The skin of your cheeks will tan,
You'll grow ragged and weary and swarthy,
   But you'll walk like a man!

Hamlin Garland

Hark to the Shouting Wind

HARK to the shouting Wind!
   Hark to the flying Rain!
And I care not though I never see
A bright blue sky again.

There are thoughts in my breast to-day
That are not for human speech;
But I hear them in the driving storm,
And the roar upon the beach.

And oh, to be with that ship
That I watched through the blinding brine!
O Wind! for thy sweepy land and sea!
O Sea! for a voice like thine!

Shout on, thou pitiless Wind,
To the frightened and flying Rain!
I care not though I never see
A calm blue sky again.

Henry Timrod

Who Has Seen the Wind?

WHO has seen the wind?
    Neither I nor you:
But when the leaves hang trembling,
    The wind is passing thro'.

Who has seen the wind?
    Neither you nor I:
But when the trees bow down their heads,
    The wind is passing by.

Christina Rossetti

Wind

WIND, wind—heather gipsy
    Whistling in my tree!
All the heart of me is tipsy
On the sound of thee.
Sweet with scent of clover,
Salt with breath of sea,
Wind, wind—wayman lover,
Whistling in my tree!

John Galsworthy

The Sea-Wind

WINNOW me through with thy keen clear breath,
  Wind with the tang of the sea!
Speed through the closing gates of day,
  Find me, and fold me, and have thy way,
And take thy will of me!

Use my soul as you use the sky,—
  Gray sky of this sullen day!
Clear its doubt as you speed its wrack
  Of storm-clouds burning its splendor back,
Giving it gold for gray!

Bring me word of the moving ships,
  Halyards and straining spars;
Come to me clear from the sea's wide breast
  While the last lights die in the yellow west
Under the first white stars!

Batter the closed doors of my heart
  And set my spirit free!
For I stifle here in this crowded place
  Sick for the tenantless fields of space,
Wind with the tang of the sea!

Arthur Ketchum

I Meant To Do My Work To-day

I MEANT to do my work to-day—
  But a brown bird sang in the apple-tree
And a butterfly flitted across the field,
  And all the leaves were calling me.

And the wind went sighing over the land,
  Tossing the grasses to and fro,
And a rainbow held out its shining hand—
  So what could I do but laugh and go?
                    Richard Le Gallienne

That Wind Is Best

WHICHEVER way the wind doth blow
  Some heart is glad to have it so;
Then blow it east or blow it west,
The wind that blows, that wind is best.

Then, whatsoever wind doth blow,
My heart is glad to have it so;
And blow it east or blow it west,
The wind that blows, that wind is best.
                    Caroline Atherton Mason

Happy Wind

OH, happy wind, how sweet
  Thy life must be!
The great, proud fields of gold
  Run after thee:
And here are flowers, with heads
  To nod and shake;
And dreaming butterflies
  To tease and wake.
Oh, happy wind, I say,
To be alive this day.

                    William H. Davies

Wind-Litany

IN this world I shall not find
Any Comforter like Wind,
Any friend to so endure,
Any love so strong, so sure.
I was born when Wind with Star
Linked its magic, and from far
Whispered out my destiny—
And the Winds have brothered me.

Strong young hill-winds roistering
Up the steep with me and Spring,
Wild wet thrilling ocean-gales
Flinging out my swelling sails,
Or the little dawning-airs
Rising pure as baby-prayers—
These have loved me since my birth
On the wind-swept swinging earth.

Rose-perfumed night-air that slips
Like a kiss across my lips,
Smoke-tanged wood-breath—they can sweep
All old childhood from its sleep
Underneath thick-fallen days
Heaped and dun across my ways;
For until the end shall be,
Scent o' wind is Memory.

I remember when befell
Heartbreak fierce, intolerable,
And no voice or touch but bound
Deeper torment on the wound:
Yet a little wind could rise
Stroking cheek and tear-wet eyes,

Breathing, "Hush! All pain shall pass!
Still are winds, and skies, and grass!"

God, when all of earth shall lie
Stripped and new beneath Thine eye,
And Thy gold stars fall unstrung,
And Thy curtain-sky down-flung,
And Thy seas are lifted up
Whole from out their empty cup,
Grant me still, in Heaven's place
Sweet swift winds across my face!

Margaret Widdemer

A Morning

THE glad, mad wind went singing by,
   The white clouds drove athwart the blue,
Bold beauty of the morning sky
   And all the world was sun and dew,
And sweet cold air with sudden glints of gold
Like spilled stars glowing in the cedars' hold.

I laughed for very joy of life,
   Oh, thrilling veins, oh, happy heart,
Of this glad world with beauty rife,
   Exult that we too are a part;
Rejoice! Rejoice! that miracle of birth
Gave us this golden heritage of earth.

Oh, bold, blue sky, oh, keen, glad wind,
   I wonder me if this may be,
That some day, leaving life behind,

Our eyes shall view new land, new sea
So exquisite that, lo! with thrilling breath,
We shall laugh loud for very joy of death.
Theodosia Garrison

The Wind's Life

I LOVE the silver-shaken,
  The windy tops of trees
That heave and lift in sequence,
  Like running surf of seas,

With swathes of changing purples
  And vistas golden-deep
Where, for an unstirred moment,
  The sunlight lies asleep.
Harry Kemp

The Mystic

I HAVE ridden the wind,
  I have ridden the sea,
I have ridden the moon and stars.
I have set my feet in the stirrup seat
Of a comet coursing Mars.
And everywhere
Thro' the earth and air
My thought speeds, lightning-shod,
It comes to a place where checking pace
It cries, "Beyond lies God!"
.   .   .   .

I have ridden the wind,
I have ridden the night,
I have ridden the ghosts that flee
From the vaults of death like a chilling breath
Over eternity.
And everywhere
Is the world laid bare—
Ether and star and clod—
Until I wind to its brink and find
But the cry, "Beyond lies God!"
.   .   .   .

I have ridden the wind,
I have ridden the stars,
I have ridden the force that flies
With far intent thro' the firmament
And each to each allies.
And everywhere
That a thought may dare
To gallop, mine has trod—
Only to stand at last on the strand
Where just beyond lies God.

Cale Young Rice

The Hillborn

Climb

My shoes fall on the house-top that is so far beneath me,
  I have hung my hat forever on the sharp church spire,
Now what shall seem the hill but a moment of surmounting,
  The height but a place to dream of something higher!

Wings? Oh not for me, I need no other pinions
  Than the beating of my heart within my breast;
Wings are for the dreamer with a bird-like longing,
  Whose dreams come home at eventide to nest.

The timid folk beseech me, the wise ones warn me,
  They say that I shall never grow to stand so high;
But I climb among the hills of cloud and follow vanished lightning,
I shall stand knee-deep in thunder with my head against the sky

Tiptoe, at last, upon a pinnacle of sunset,
  I shall greet the death-like evening with laughter from afar,
Nor tremble in the darkness nor shun the windy midnight,
  For by the evening I shall be a star.

Winifred Welles

The Mountain Sat

THE mountain sat upon the plain
 In his eternal chair,
His observation omnifold,
His inquest everywhere.

The seasons prayed around his knees,
Like children round a sire:
Grandfather of the days is he,
Of dawn the ancestor.

Emily Dickinson

One Kind of Humility

SHALL we say heaven is not heaven
 Since golden stairs are rugged and uneven?

Or that no light illuminates a star
That swings in other regions than we are?

Deny with soured breath enduring God
Because we cling so rankly to the sod?

No. Cleanse with weeping, fasting and with prayer.
Praise God. Look starward. Mount the stair!

Jean Starr Untermeyer

The Cry of the Hillborn

I AM homesick for the mountains—
My heroic mother hills—
And the longing that is on me
No solace ever stills.

I would climb to brooding summits
With their old untarnished dreams,
Cool my heart in forest shadows
To the lull of falling streams;

Hear the innocence of aspens
That babble in the breeze,
And the fragrant sudden showers
That patter on the trees.

I am lonely for my thrushes
In their hermitage withdrawn,
Toning the quiet transports
Of twilight and of dawn.

I need the pure, strong mornings,
When the soul of day is still,
With the touch of frost that kindles
The scarlet on the hill;

Lone trails and winding woodroads
To outlooks wild and high,
And the pale moon waiting sundown
Where ledges cut the sky.

I dream of upland clearings
Where cones of sumac burn,

And gaunt and gray-mossed boulders
Lie deep in beds of fern;

The gray and mottled beeches,
The birches' satin sheen,
The majesty of hemlocks
Crowning the blue ravine.

My eyes dim for the skyline
Where purple peaks aspire,
And the forges of the sunset
Flare up in golden fire.

There crests look down unheeding
And see the great winds blow,
Tossing the huddled tree-tops
In gorges far below;

Where cloud-mists from the warm earth
Roll up about their knees,
And hang their filmy tatters
Like prayers upon the trees.

I cry for night-blue shadows
On plain and hill and dome,—
The spell of old enchantments,
The sorcery of home.

Bliss Carman

Up a Hill and a Hill

UP a hill and a hill there's a sudden orchard-slope,
And a little tawny field in the sun;

There's a gray wall that coils like a twist of frayed-out rope,
   And grasses nodding news one to one.

Up a hill and a hill there's a windy place to stand,
   And between the apple-boughs to find the blue
Of the sleepy summer sea, past the cliffs of orange sand,
   With the white charmed ships sliding through.

Up a hill and a hill there's a little house as gray
   As a stone that the glaciers scored and stained;
With a red rose by the door, and a tangled garden-way,
   And a face at the window, checker-paned.

I could climb, I could climb, till the shoes fell off my feet,
   Just to find that tawny field above the sea!
Up a hill and a hill,—oh, the honeysuckle's sweet!
   And the eyes at the window watch for me!

Fannie Stearns Davis

Hills

I NEVER loved your plains!—
   Your gentle valleys,
Your drowsy country lanes
   And pleachèd alleys.

I want my hills!—the trail
   That scorns the hollow.—
Up, up the ragged shale
   Where few will follow,

Up, over wooded crest
   And mossy boulder

With strong thigh, heaving chest,
  And swinging shoulder,

So let me hold my way,
  By nothing halted,
Until, at close of day,
  I stand, exalted,

High on my hills of dream—
  Dear hills that know me!
And then, how fair will seem
  The lands below me,

How pure, at vesper-time,
  The far bells chiming!
God, give me hills to climb,
  And strength for climbing!

Arthur Guiterman

Again Among the Hills

AGAIN among the hills!
  The shaggy hills!
The clear arousing air comes like a call
Of bugle notes across the pines, and thrills
My heart as if a hero had just spoken.
Again among the hills!
The jubilant, unbroken,
Long dreaming of the hills!
Far off, Ascutney smiles as one at peace;
And over all
The golden sunlight pours, and fills
The hollow of the earth, like a god's joy.

Again among the hills!
The tranquil hills
That took me as a boy
And filled my spirit with the silences!

O indolent, far-reaching hills that lie
Secure in your own strength, and take your ease
Like careless giants 'neath the summer sky—
What is it to you, O hills,
That anxious men should take thought for the morrow?
What has your might to do with thought or sorrow,
Or cark and cumber of conflicting wills?
Lone Pine, that thron'st thyself upon the height,
Aloof and kingly, overlooking all,
Yet uncompanioned, with the Day and Night
For pageant and the winds for festival!
I was thy minion once, and now renew
Mine ancient fealty—
To that which shaped me still remaining true,
And through allegiance only growing free.

. . . .

The rising of the wind among the pines,
The runic wind, full of old legendries!
It talks to the ancient trees
Of sights and signs
And strange earth-creatures strong to make or mar—
Such tales as when the firelight flickered out
In the old days men heard and had no doubt.
O wind, what is your spell?
Borne on your cry, the ages slip away,
And lo, I too am of that elder day;
I crouch by the logs and hear
With credent ear
And simple marvel the far tales men tell.

. . . .

. . . Night on the hills!
And the ancient stars emerge.
The silence of their mighty distances
Compels the world to peace. Now sinks the surge
Of life to a soft stir of mountain rills,
And over the swarm and urge
Of eager men sleep falls and darkling ease.

Night on the hills!
Dark mother-Night, draw near;
Lay hands on us and whisper words of cheer
So softly, oh, so softly! Now may we
Be each as one that leaves his midnight task
And throws his casement open; and the air
Comes up across the lowlands from the sea
And cools his temples, as a maid might ask
With shy caress what speech would never dare;
And he leans back to her demure desires,
And as a dream sees far below
The city with its lights aglow
And blesses in his heart his brothers there;
Then toward the eternal stars again aspires.
Richard Hovey

Hill Hunger

I WANT to stride the hills! My feet cry out
For hills! Oh, I am sick to death of streets:
The nausea of pavements and people always about;
The savagery of mortar and steel that beats
Me under, hedges me in; the iron shiver
Of traffic!—I want to stride the hills, I want
Hills toned frantic silver or a quiver

Of scarlet; hills that hunger and grow gaunt!
I am tired of steps and steps, and a thousand flights
Of stairs resounding, shuffling, quarreling
With shoes. I want a hill on windy nights,
When April pauses with me, clambering
Over the purple side to the top, until
We pull ourselves up by a star—the hill! the hill!
Joseph Auslander

Afternoon on a Hill

I WILL be the gladdest thing
  Under the sun!
I will touch a hundred flowers
  And not pick one.

I will look at cliffs and clouds
  With quiet eyes,
Watch the wind bow down the grass,
  And the grass rise.

And when lights begin to show
  Up from the town,
I will mark which must be mine,
  And then start down!

Edna St. Vincent Millay

The Hills

O MY Soul, let us go unto our hills,
  We were native to them one day, you and I—
Less dwellers of the earth than of the sky

Where the holy sense of silence stays and stills,
  Like a hand of benediction lifted high.

We have stayed in this market-place too long;
  We have bartered with the birth-right in our breast;
  We have shamed us with buffoonery and jest,
Nor raised our eyes to where our hills were strong,
  Above this petty region of unrest.

O, my Soul, let us go unto our hills,
  To their wonderful, high silence and their might,
  Where the old dreams shall whisper us by night
Till the sullen heart within us stirs and thrills,
  And wakes to weep and wonder and delight.
O my soul, let us go unto our hills.

Theodosia Garrison

On a Hill

SPRING on a wind-swept hill!
  The grass at our feet
Sheered into waves of light!
Spring, and the woodbird's trill!
Spring, and the stars of night
Turned dewdrops glist'ning sweet.
Earth-chained we stand,
Thinking unearthly things,
Looking across the land,
Over the hills, beyond the sea,
Our souls on tireless wings
    Soaring Eternity.

Spring! oh, the wind's rush
In the joyous trees!

> Oh, wide, free sky, and white
> Laughing clouds! And the hush
> When, as a musician's might,
> God's Hand rests on His keys.
>
> *Irene Rutherford McLeod*

The Most-Sacred Mountain

SPACE, and the twelve clean winds of heaven,
And this sharp exultation, like a cry, after the slow six thousand steps of climbing!
This is Tai Shan, the beautiful, the most holy.

Below my feet the foot-hills nestle, brown with flecks of green; and lower down the flat brown plain, the floor of earth, stretches away to blue infinity.
Beside me in this airy space the temple roofs cut their slow curves against the sky,
And one black bird circles above the void.

Space, and the twelve clean winds are here;
And with them broods eternity—a swift, white peace, a presence manifest.
The rhythm ceases here. Time has no place. This is the end that has no end.

Here, when Confucius came, a half a thousand years before the Nazarene, he stepped, with me, thus into timelessness.
The stone beside us waxes, old the carven stone that says: "On this spot once Confucius stood and felt the smallness of the world below."
The stone grows old:
Eternity is not for stones.
But I shall go down from this airy place, this swift white peace, this stinging exultation.

And time will close about me, and my soul stir to the rhythm
of the daily round.
Yet, having known, life will not press so close, and always I
shall feel time ravel thin about me;
For once I stood
In the white windy presence of eternity.

Eunice Tietjens

Traveler's Joy

Sea-Chill

I MUST go down to the seas again, where the billows romp and reel,
So all I ask is a large ship that rides on an even keel,
And a mild breeze and a broad deck with a slight list to leeward,
And a clean chair in a snug nook and a nice, kind steward.

I must go down to the seas again, the sport of wind and tide,
As the gray wave and the green wave play leapfrog over the side.
And all I want is a glassy calm with a bone-dry scupper,
A good book and a warm rug and a light, plain supper.

I must go down to the seas again, though there I'm a total loss,
And can't say which is worst, the pitch, the plunge, the roll, the toss.
But all I ask is a safe retreat in a bar well tended,
And a soft berth and a smooth course till the long trip's ended.

Arthur Guiterman

Bring Me the Sunset in a Cup

BRING me the sunset in a cup,
    Reckon the morning's flagons up,
  And say how many dew;
Tell me how far the morning leaps,
Tell me what time the weaver sleeps
  Who spun the breadths of blue!

Write me how many notes there be
In the new robin's ecstasy
  Among astonished boughs;
How many trips the tortoise makes,
How many cups the bee partakes,—
  The debauchee of dews!

Also, who laid the rainbow's piers,
Also, who leads the docile spheres
  By withes of supple blue?
Whose fingers string the stalactite,
Who counts the wampum of the night,
  To see that none is due?

Who built this little Alban house
And shut the windows down so close
  My spirit cannot see?
Who'll let me out some gala day,
With implements to fly away,
  Passing pomposity?

Emily Dickinson

Traveller's Joy

WHAT went you, Pilgrim, for to see?
    A sign or wonder-thing maybe?
Some marvel or a holy sight
As clerks in chronicles do write?
For you have gone and come again,
Now tell us plain?

I saw the sky from rim to rim
Full-filled with light up to the brim,
As though it were a mighty cup
To God's lip holden up.
I saw a river and a down,
A harbor and a little town,
A marshland blue with irises—
I saw all these.

Saw, too, a sedgy pond where lay
Lilies like anchored stars that Day
Had ravished from the summer night
And kept them there alight.
I saw a hill-side gold with furze,
And wildrose banks and junipers
Distilling fragrance pungent-sweet;
I saw a path that called my feet
To go with it as any friend,
To heart's desire at the end.

Sooth, all of these! but 'mid them all
Did nothing wonderful befall?
No miracle?
Yea, but I have no word to tell
Of that great thing that happened me—
I saw the sea!

O wide, and blue and infinite!
League upon league of space and light!
I think that down this sapphire floor
One might walk straight to heaven's door
And lift its golden latchet-bar,
Nor find it far
Or very strange, as one would guess,
After such earthly loveliness.

Poor pilgrim, is this all your store
Of tales to tell? Is there no more
Than this that any man might show?
Yea, all is told. How should you know
That I have looked on Beauty's face,
And being far from men a space
Have found at springs of Quietness
The hands that heal, the hands that bless—
Have known the sun and wind and trod
The holy earth and talked with God!
Arthur Ketchum

Ellis Park

LITTLE park that I pass through,
I carry off a piece of you
Every morning hurrying down
To my work-day in the town;
Carry you for country there
To make the city ways more fair.

I take your trees
And your breeze,
Your greenness,
Your cleanness,
Some of your shade, some of your sky,

Some of your calm as I go by;
Your flowers to trim
The pavements grim;
Your space for room in the jostled street,
And grass for carpet to my feet.
Your fountains take and sweet bird calls
To sing me from my office walls.
All that I can see
I carry off with me.

But you never miss my theft,
So much treasures you have left.
As I find you, fresh at morning,
So I find you, home returning,
Nothing lacking from your grace.
All your riches wait in place
For me to borrow
On the morrow.

Do you hear this praise of you,
Little park that I pass through?

Helen Hoyt

Afoot

LONG is the road 'twixt town and town that runs,
    Travelled by many a lordly cavalcade,
With trappings gay, and rich caparisons,
   Jester and squire, and laughing knight and maid:
With gallant clash and stir they go their way:
I trudge afoot thro' all the drouth of day.

For me, the misty meadows fresh with morn,
   The tramp thro' noontide heat to evening gray,

The far-seen smoke from the day's goal upborne,
   The halt, the friendly greeting by the way,
The distant hill beyond far hill descried,
The road by day, the rest at eventide.

I know each wayside wood, each moorland brown,
   Each hidden by-way and reposeful nook,
Where I may linger when the sun goes down,
   Dipping tired feet in some cool flowing brook;
I know the free hill and the glooming glen,
And kindly fires, and humble homes of men.
                                           C. Fox-Smith

The Going of His Feet

HIS feet went here and there
   About the common earth.
He touched to grandeur all
   Men held of little worth.

He loved the growing flowers,
   The small bright singing birds,
The patient flocks of sheep,
   The many-pastured herds.

The field of rippling corn
   That shimmered in the sun,
The soft blue smoke of eve
   That curled when day was done. . . .

He did not search afar
   For what He had to say:
His mind reached forth and drew
   Its strength from every day:

The struggling nets, alive
  With fish drawn from the sea
Supplied Him with the apt
  And chosen simile. . . .

He saw a neighbor build
  A house that did not stand—
And men may not forget
  The House Upon The Sand;

He saw a widow drop
  Her mite into the hoard—
And to eternity
  That treasure is up-stored;

He heard a publican
  Who thought none others there—
The souls of all mankind
  Are richer for that prayer. . . .

O, Poet of the World,
  I pray Thee, come to me,
That my lame heart might walk,
  That my dark soul may see;

And teach me, too, to go
  About the ways of earth
And find the Wealth of God
  In things of little worth!

Harry Kemp

Down East and Up Along

DOWN east and up along the fringy coast of Maine
  There's rumor of the summer and the warm soft rain.
There's lisp of little leaves astir in the heart of every tree,

There's gossip in the grasses that run down to meet the sea.
In my heart I hear them calling like a siren's song,
"Come and share the glories of down east and up along!"

Down east and up along the brooks are flowing full,
The gray sea is blue again, the spring tides pull,
The keening of the winter wind no longer haunts the seas,
There's the velvet touch of raindrops upon the southern breeze.
The throb of life resurgent is calling loud and long,
"Come and share the glories of down east and up along!"

Down east and up along the sun is warm again,
Calling to the hungry hearts of city-weary men.
Telling of the golden days in a land of woods and sea,
A land of summer glory and of autumn ecstasy.
You can almost hear the music of the hovering angel throng,
For the very edge of Heaven lies down east and up along!
Edwin Osgood Grover

The Joys of the Road

NOW the joys of the road are chiefly these:
A crimson touch on the hard-wood trees;

A vagrant's morning wide and blue,
In early fall, when the wind walks, too;

A shadowy highway cool and brown,
Alluring up and enticing down

From rippled water to dappled swamp,
From purple glory to scarlet pomp;

The outward eye, the quiet will,
And the striding hart from hill to hill;

The tempter apple over the fence;
The cobweb bloom on the yellow quince;

The palish asters along the wood,
A lyric touch of the solitude;

An open hand, an easy shoe,
And a hope to make the day go through,—

Another to sleep with, and a third
To wake me up at the voice of a bird;

The resonant, far-listening morn,
And the hoarse whisper of the corn;

The crickets mourning their comrades lost,
In the night's retreat from the gathering frost

(Or is it their slogan, plaintive and shrill,
As they beat on their corselets, valiant still?)

A hunger fit for the kings of the sea,
And a loaf of bread for Dickon and me;

A thirst like that of the Thirsty Sword,
And a jug of cider on the board;

An idle noon, a bubbling spring,
The sea in the pine-tops murmuring;

A scrap of gossip at the ferry;
A comrade neither glum nor merry,

Asking nothing, revealing naught,
But minting his words from a fund of thought,

A keeper of silence eloquent,
Needy, yet royally well content,

Of the mettled breed, yet abhorring strife,
And full of the mellow juice of life,

No fidget and no reformer, just
A calm observer of ought and must,

A lover of books, but a reader of man,
No cynic and no charlatan,

Who never defers and never demands,
But smiling, takes the world in his hands,—

Seeing it good as when God first saw
And gave it the weight of His will for law.

And Oh, the joy that is never won,
But follows and follows the journeying sun,

By marsh and tide, by meadow and stream,
A will-o'-the-wisp, a light-o'-dream,

Delusion afar, delight anear,
From morrow to morrow, from year to year,

A jack-o'-lantern, a fairy fire,
A dare, a bliss, and a desire!

The racy smell of the forest loam,
When the stealthy, sad-heart leaves go home;

(O leaves, O leaves, I am one with you,
Of the mould and the sun and the wind and the dew!)

The broad gold wake of the afternoon;
The silent fleck of the cold new moon;

The sound of the hollow sea's release
From stormy tumult to starry peace;

With only another league to wend;
And two brown arms at the journey's end!

These are the joys of the open road—
For him who travels without a load.

Bliss Carman

Song of the Open

THERE'S a whisper in the orchard, there's a laughter
    in the breeze,
There's a catbird's chuckle in the maple tree;
And the wind has come from westward, scattering the
    maple-keys.
Oh, it's time to break your fetters and be free!

All the rain's astir and calling, all the grass is wet and
    brown,
All the world waits just beyond the window-pane;
And the day is dull and dripping in the gray, gas-lighted
    town,
But the country's fresh and clean with fall again.

Oh, it's out along the prairie with the cool rain in your
    face,

And it's out along the river flowing free,
And it's out across the hill-tops in a flying-footed race
With just your heart to bear you company.

There's the prairie curving softly with its golden blooms aglow,
And the purple splashes on its ripened flanks;
And the idle grassy hollows where the brilliant salvias grow,
And the sturdy cat-tails marshal out their ranks.

Ah, the scarlet of the orchards and the saffron of the fields!
Ah, the purple of the vineyards in the sun!
Ah, the river in the sunlight, flashing silver as a shield
For a moment—and your Indian summer's done.

So it's home along the prairie with the north wind blowing chill,
And it's home across the meadow's heaving sea,
And it's home with winter shouting just beyond the farthest hill,
But yet the road is open and is free.

Sara Hamilton Birchall

Rebellion

TO wake at morn,
   And hear the little laugh
Of the lake-wind in the trees;
  To watch at dawn
The earliest sunbeam kiss
The mist-crowned, towering peaks
And glide down to the plains.

Ah, that is Life!
Not this—
 To wake at morn,
And hear the swelling roar
Of Man, Beast and Machine,
Toiling in murky air
 And a city's sweat!

 At noon to dream
Where Nature's bowers are hid
 Beneath an arch
Of twined and intersticing vines,
 While on the air
Quivers the chanting of the sighing woods,
And the songs of mating birds.

 Ah, that is Life!
Not this—
 At noon to pause,
And lay aside the pen for one brief hour:
Then to return, as I did yesterday,
Will do to-morrow and on all to-morrows—
 Oh, Fool, Machine, and Slave!

 Again at dusk,
To watch the sun's last ray
 Fade in the west;
To feel Earth's grand transition
 From day to night—
That moment when the world
Pauses and knows itself!
 The Angelus chimes
And echoes round the Earth;

 Here the Muezzin's call,
 There a child's lullaby,

And now a poor serf's prayer. . . .
   Earth's evensong!

To hear that is to live!
   Not this—
To breast the roaring surge
Of thousands, pale and tired, dead in soul,
Crowding with merciless haste toward home.
Home? . . .
Past ere the sweet of home has touched the sense!
To toil that we may sleep
   That better we may toil;
To toil that we may eat,
   That better we may toil.
Ay, that is Life; but still—
   But still we dream!

Stephen Chalmers

The Tree-Top Road

LIFE'S sweetest joys are hidden
   In unsubstantial things;
An April rain, a fragrance,
   A vision of blue wings:
And what are memory and hope
   But dreams? And yet the bread
On which these little lives of ours
   Are fed and comforted!

Without imagination
   The soul becomes a clod,
Missing the trail of beauty,
   Losing the way to God.
And I have built a templed-stair

Out of a lilac bloom
And climbed to heaven with purple pomp
And censers of perfume!

. . . .

I have no feud with Labor,
But at the Gates of June
I fling away my dusty pack
And join in Youth's glad tune.
And just forgetting for a while
That I am worn and gray,
Go sailing off with Peter Pan
Along the Tree-top Way!

May Riley Smith

Early Morning at Bargis

CLEAR air and grassy lea,
Stream-song and cattle-bell—
Dear man, what fools are we
In prison-walls to dwell!

To live our days apart
From green things and wide skies,
And let the wistful heart
Be cut and crushed with lies!

Bright peaks!—And suddenly
Light floods the placid dell,
The grass-tops brush my knee:
A good crop it will be,
So all is well!
O man, what fools are we
In prison-walls to dwell!

Hermann Hagedorn

Denial

IT is not down this road I walk,
 Or through these brown-leaved trees;
For in my heart I loiter where
 The clover calls the bees;

Where trees are green and streams are warm,
 And drowsy life is sweet—
It is not down this lane I go
 With tired, reluctant feet.

Lancaster Pollard

"*A La Belle Ètoile*"

OH, who will lodge at my Inn tonight,
 And live both fair and fine,
With a blossoming blackberry vine for a gate,
And a friendly star for a sign?

Good sir, my Inn is a gentle Inn,
The wine is sweet and old;
'Tis Adam's, sir, with a fine bouquet,
And the color of liquid gold.

The carriages roll on the rocky road
To a musty house afar;
But the gentlefolk stop by the blackberry gate
At the Inn of the Beautiful Star.

Sweet fern, sweet fern for your pillow, sir,
And a quick-eared faun for your mate,

And a firefly's light for your candle bright—
Good sooth, we sleep in state.

The winds go murmuring by at dusk
And call you up at dawn,
To walk through the fairies' handkerchiefs
And startle a sleeping fawn.

When day is red on the river's bed,
And bright on quartz and spar,
We'll say our short St. Martin's grace
At the Inn of the Beautiful Star.

The blackberry vine is a maiden now,
With her pale stars in the dew;
Come back next month, good sir, there'll be
Sweet blackberries for you.

We'll wish you luck from the blackberry gate.
Although you wander far,
'Tis here that you'll come home at last—
To our Inn of the Beautiful Star.
Sara Hamilton Birchall

Journey

AH, could I lay me down in this long grass
And close my eyes, and let the quiet wind
Blow over me,—I am so tired, so tired
Of passing pleasant places! All my life,
Following Care along the dusty road,
Have I looked back at loveliness and sighed;
Yet at my hand an unrelenting hand
Tugged ever, and I passed. All my life long

Over my shoulder have I looked at peace;
And now I fain would lie in this long grass
And close my eyes,
       Yet onward!

                Cat-birds call
Through the long afternoon, and creeks at dusk
Are guttural. Whippoorwills wake and cry,
Drawing the twilight close about their throats.
Only my heart makes answer. Eager vines
Go up the rocks and wait; flushed apple-trees
Pause in their dance and break the ring for me;
Dim, shady wood-roads, redolent of fern
And bayberry, that through sweet bevies thread
Of round-faced roses, pink and petulant,
Look back and beckon ere they disappear.
Only my heart, only my heart responds,
Yet, ah, my path is sweet on either side
All through the dragging day,—sharp underfoot,
And hot, and like dead mist the dry dust hangs—
But far, oh, far as passionate eye can reach,
And long, ah, long as rapturous eye can cling,
The world is mine; blue hill, still silver lake,
Broad field, bright flower, and the long white road.
A gateless garden, and an open path;
My feet to follow, and my heart to hold.
                    Edna St. Vincent Millay

The Sojourner

I WILL arise and go; the wind is fain of me,
  The laughing wind that stirs my climbing rose;
The tiny clusters nod and talk together,
But what their secret may be, no one knows.

I will arise and go; the wind is fain of me,
The rose is heavy in the southern town,
The wild geese travel northward in the mornings,
The bold-eyed southern spring tears wide her gown.

I will arise and go; the wind is fain of me,
The last snow melts beneath the gray stone walls,
The green young sedges fringe the river-margin,
And in my heart the Northland calls and calls.

I will arise and go; the wind is fain of me.
Too long I wait in summer's tasselled hall,
Too long I dream amid the tulip blossoms,
Too long I linger when I hear the call.

I will arise and go to seek the mountains,
I will return my playfellows to greet;
Once more the open hills and the sweet meadow,
Once more the virgin Northland's lips to meet.
                                Sara Hamilton Birchall

Traveller's Rest

WHEN you are tired of the long road and the open sky,
  I wish it may be my door that you're passing by:
I wish it may be my hearth where you will sit down
And tell your tales of the land and sea and the strange
    far town.

Oh, come you in from eastward or come you in from the
    west,
Here's good cheer to greet you and welcome of the best:

Oh, come you with your pockets full or come you home
    poor,
Here's a place by the fireside and an open door.

You'll tell me where you were since, and the things you've
    seen
Up and down the wide world where so long you've been,—
All the time that I've been here and you far away,—
And then awhile be silent, as good friends may.

And then awhile listen to the wind and rain,
Moaning in the chimney-breast, beating at the pane,—
Dark and cold outside there, and the stormy skies,
And you sitting down here with the firelight in your eyes.
                                        C. Fox-Smith

Far From the Madding Crowd

IT seems to me I'd like to go
    Where bells don't ring nor whistles blow,
Nor clocks don't strike nor gongs don't sound,
But where there's stillness all around.

Not real still stillness; just the trees'
Low whisperings or the croon of bees;
The drowsy tinklings of the rill,
Or twilight song of whippoorwill.

'Twould be a joy could I behold
The dappled fields of green and gold,
Or in the cool, sweet clover lie
And watch the cloud-ships drifting by.

I'd like to find some quaint old boat,
And fold its oars, and with it float
Along the lazy, limpid stream
Where water-lilies drowse and dream.

Sometimes it seems to me I must
Just quit the city's din and dust,
For fields of green and skies of blue;
And, say! How does it seem to you?
Nixon Waterman

Streams

I SO love water-laughter,
 Its bubbling flecks and gleams,
I pray in the hereafter
 There somewhere may be streams.

I'd have for my companion
 In some celestial nook,
Beneath a spreading banyan,
 The music of a brook.

Its measures would entice me,
 Uncumbered by the clay,
Its melody suffice me
 Till drooped the heavenly day.

Then its all-liquid laughter
 Would murmur through my dreams;
I pray in the hereafter
 There somewhere may be streams.
Clinton Scollard

The Call

I MUST get out to the woods again, to the whispering
    tree and the birds awing,
Away from the haunts of pale-faced men, to the spaces wide
    where strength is king;
I must get out where the skies are blue and the air is clean
    and the rest is sweet,
Out where there's never a task to do or a goal to reach or
    a foe to meet.

I must get out on the trails once more that wind through
    shadowy haunts and cool,
Away from the presence of wall and door, and see myself
    in a crystal pool;
I must get out with the silent things, where neither laughter
    nor hate is heard,
Where malice never the humblest stings and no one is hurt
    by a spoken word.

Oh, I've heard the call of the tall white pine, and heard
    the call of the running brook,
I'm tired of the tasks which each day are mine, I'm weary
    of reading a printed book,
I want to get out of the din and strife, the clank and
    clamor of turning wheel,
And walk for a day where life is life, and the joys are
    true and the pictures real.

Edgar A. Guest

The Road that Leads to Home

MY road is a by-road, with big trees reaching high,
    A tapestry of living green against a sapphire sky;

An olden road, a golden road, is the road I love to roam
A gleaming road, a dreaming road, the road that leads to home.

My road is a shy road, where whispering lovers stray
And breathe the scent of the bramble-rose and fields of new-mown hay;
A road to woo with a song or two, ere the day has yet begun,
A smiling road, a beguiling road, that dips into the sun.

My road is a by-road, where townfolk never tread,
With wild wind flowers in the grass, and green leaves overhead;
Oh, dawn-mist road, oh, star-kissed road, across the white sea foam
I hear you crying, hear you sighing, calling the wand'rer home.

Ethel E. Mannin

Where Lies the Land?

WHERE lies the land to which the ship would go?
    Far, far ahead, is all her seamen known.
And where the land she travels from? Away,
Far, far behind, is all that they can say.

On sunny noons upon the deck's smooth face,
Linked arm in arm, how pleasant here to pace;
Or, o'er the stern reclining, watch below
The foaming wake far widening as we go.

On stormy nights when wild northwesters rave,
How proud a thing to fight with wind and wave!
The dripping sailor on the reeling mast
Exults to bear, and scorns to wish it past.

Where lies the land to which the ship would go?
Far, far ahead, is all her seamen know.
And where the land she travels from? Away,
Far, far behind, is all that they can say.
Arthur Hugh Clough

Echoes from Vagabondia

Song of the Open Road

I THINK that I shall never see
A billboard lovely as a tree.
Perhaps, unless the billboards fall,
I'll never see a tree at all.

Ogden Nash

The Fiddling Lad

"THERE'LL be no roof to shelter you;
You'll have no where to lay your head.
And who will get your food for you?
  Star-dust pays for no man's bread.
    So, Jacky, come give me your fiddle
    If ever you mean to thrive."
"I'll have the skies to shelter me,
  The green grass it shall be my bed,
And happen I'll find somewhere for me
  A sup of drink, a bit of bread;
    And I'll not give my fiddle
    To any man alive."

And it's out he went across the wold,
  His fiddle tucked beneath his chin,
And (golden bow on silver strings)
  Smiling he fiddled the twilight in;
And fiddled in the frosty moon,
  And all the stars of the Milky Way,
And fiddled low through the dark of dawn,
  And laughed and fiddled in the day.

But oh, he had no bit nor sup,
  And oh, the winds blew stark and cold,
And when he dropped on his grass-green bed
  It's long he slept on the open wold.
They digged his grave and, "There," they said,
  "He's got more land than ever he had,
And well it will keep him held and housed,
  The feckless bit of a fiddling lad."

And it's out he's stepped across the wold
  His fiddle tucked beneath his chin—
A wavering shape in the wavering light,
  Smiling he fiddles the twilight in,
And fiddles in the frosty moon,
  And all the stars of the Milky Way,
And fiddles low through the dark of dawn,
  And laughs and fiddles in the day.

He needeth not or bit or sup,
  The winds of night he need not fear,
And (bow of gold on silver strings)
  It's all the peoples turn to hear.
"Oh never," it's all the people cry,
  "Came such sweet sounds from mortal hand";
And, "Listen," they say, "it's some ghostly boy
  That goes a-fiddling through the land.

Hark you! It's night comes slipping in,—
  The moon and the stars that tread the sky;
And there's the breath of the world that stops;
  And now with a shout the sun comes by!"
Who heareth him he heedeth not
  But smiles content, the fiddling lad;
He murmurs, "Oh many's the happy day,
My fiddle and I together have had;
  And could I give my fiddle
  To any man alive?"

Adelaide Crapsey

Wanderthirst

BEYOND the East the sunrise, beyond the West the sea,
And East and West the wanderthirst that will not let me be;
It works in me like madness, to bid me say good-bye;
For the seas call and the stars call, and oh! the call of the sky.

I know not where the white road runs, nor what the blue hills are,
But a man can have the Sun for friend, and for his guide a star;
And there's no end of voyaging when once the voice is heard,
For the river calls and the road calls, and oh! the call of a bird!

Yonder the long horizon lies, and there by night and day
The old ships draw to home again, the young ships sail away;
And come I may, but go I must, and, if men ask you why,
You may put the blame on the stars and the sun and the white road and the sky.

Gerald Gould

The Vagabond

TO tread the path of glory needs a braver soul than I,
A man who will not stop to watch the white clouds drifting by,
A man who will not pause to throw a pebble in a stream
Or stretch full length upon its bank, the captive of a dream.

A braver soul than I must tread the rugged way and long,
A man who will not stop to catch the wild canary's song,
A man who'll pass a thousand charms and never turn to see
The beauty of the petaled dress upon an apple tree.

To tread the path of glory needs a stronger soul than mine,
A man that isn't tempted when the air is sharp as wine,
A man that has no vision save the golden goal he seeks,
And doesn't hear the language which the voice of nature speaks.

But I am prey to woods and fields, to sunny hills and streams,
And I've a soul which likes to drift and tease itself with dreams,
And weak am I that should be strong—a sunbeam on a pond
Has but to wink an eye at me, and I'm a vagabond.

Edgar A. Guest

Gipsy Song

GIPSY, gipsy, gipsy girl!
April's at the door,
April's whistling through the wood—
Must I call once more?

Gipsy, gipsy, gipsy girl!
Keen across the night
Hylas flutes among the pools
And the road's moon-white.

Gipsy, gipsy, gipsy girl!
Must I whistle still,

Waiting at your silent door
On the ferny hill?

Moonlit road and breaking sea,
Wet wind from the south!
Gipsy, all your lover lacks
Is your scarlet mouth!
Sara Hamilton Birchall

The Road To Vagabondia

HE was sitting on a doorstep as I went strolling by;
A lonely little beggar with a wistful, homesick eye—
And he wasn't what you'd borrow
And he wasn't what you'd steal—
But I guessed his heart was breaking,
So I whistled him to heel.

They had stoned him through the city streets and naught the city cared,
But I was heading outward and the roads are sweeter shared,
So I took him for a comrade and I whistled him away—
On the road to Vagabondia that lies across the day.

Yellow dog he was; but bless you—he was just the chap for me!
For I'd rather have an inch of dog than miles of pedigree.
So we stole away together on the road that has no end
With a new-coined day to fling away and all the stars to spend!

Oh, to walk the road at morning, when the wind is blowing clean,

And the yellow daisies fling their gold across a world of green—
For the wind it heals the heart-aches and the sun it dries the scars,
On the road to Vagabondia that lies beneath the stars.

'Twas the wonder of the going cast a spell about our feet—
We walked because the world was young, because the way was sweet;
And we slept in wild-rose meadows by the little wayside farms,
'Til the Dawn came up the highroad with the dead moon in her arms.

Oh, the Dawn it went before us through a shining lane of skies,
And the Dream was at our heartstrings and the light was in our eyes,
And we made no boast of glory and we made no boast of birth,
On the road to Vagabondia that lies across the earth.

Dana Burnet

Gipsy Feet

OH, gipsy hearts are many enough, but gipsy feet are few!
Many's the one that loves to dream night-long of stars and dew:
Many's the one that loves the scent of wood-smoke by the way,
And turns a leaping longing heart to every dawn of day.

Gipsy hearts are many enough, but gipsy feet are few.—
Ah, how ill it is to bide unloosed the long year through!
Up and down the loud gray streets, stared at, staring back,
Through tarnished trails of the staggering sun and soot-fog ochre-black;—

Dressed in heavy and sober togs, eating of heavy fare,
Hailed by only the screaming street, "Mind! step lively there!"
Crook-backed over a dusty desk,—bothering to and fro
There in the dull and airless house,—ah, to cut and go!—

Up the hill-roads into the day! Over the sea-ward fells,
Watch the thistle-down dip, and hear the thin sheep's huddling bells;
Run like fire along the field, worship the heart of the wood,
Kneel by the spring that splits the rock, and find the white rain good.

—Oh, gipsy hearts are many enough, but gipsy feet are few;
And secret gods must we worship still, if we worship fire and dew.
For we must bend at the dusty desk, and over the counter lean,—
Toil and moil in the sun-starved house, though leaves blow red or green.

God, great God of the wind's caress, God of the sea's salute,
Why are we chained and muzzled and meshed more than our brother the brute?
Shall there be never a day that all of the gipsy hearts may greet,
Laughing out at the lure of the sun for the lift of the gipsy feet?

But oh, though that day is far to come, and the feet forget
 to go free,
Pray God that the hearts may not forget the hurt and the
 ecstasy!
Pray God that never the fret may fail when the Spring
 comes over the year,
That never the thin gay autumn dawns may seem less wild
 and dear.

For shall it not be the height of Heaven, wonderful, swift,
 and sweet,
If into the paths of perilous death may wander the gipsy
 feet?
May wander free, with the risk of the road, the road that
 the glad Dead know,
Out where the fires of God flame high, and the winds of
 God lean low!

Fannie Stearns Davis

A Strip of Blue

I DO not own an inch of land,
 But all I see is mine,—
The orchard and the mowing-fields,
 The lawns and gardens fine.
The winds my tax-collectors are,
 They bring me tithes divine,—
Wild scents and subtle essences,
 A tribute rare and free;
And, more magnificent than all,
 My window keeps for me
A glimpse of blue immensity,—
 A little strip of sea.

Richer am I than he who owns
  Great fleets and argosies;
I have a share in every ship
  Won by the inland breeze
To loiter on yon airy road,
  Above the apple-trees.
I freight them with my untold dreams;
  Each bears my own picked crew;
And nobler cargoes wait for them
  Than ever India knew,—
My ships that sail into the East
  Across that outlet blue.

Lucy Larcom

Black Ashes

SOMETIME we shall remember them, the little camping places,
A day long, an hour long, a halt beside the way,
Shall see again before us the mountains' kindly faces
With the white roads pleading, leading through the hill-mists wreathing gray.

> Lichened spur and creeping trail, sun-gold in the west,
> Purple moorland, misty lure-land spreading far beneath;
> Red-gold flamelight lifting, drifting, round the pine-dark crest
> To dim the little village lights asleep upon the heath.

Sometime we shall remember them, from out the days that bind us,
A year long, a life long, that link and hold us fast,

Will come a breath of twilight blent with woodsmoke to
   remind us
Of the little camping places in the springtimes that are past.

> White-spread dunes and opal sea, gray gulls slant
>   the spray,
> Spiced sweetfern by sandy turn where the sun strikes
>   gold,
> Scent of woodsmoke, vagrant, fragrant, ah, it haunts
>   the air today
> From the little camping places in the Story That
>   Is Told.

Martha Haskell Clark

The Wander Lure

THE robin's on the wing again; I hear the call o' spring
   again,
   And fain am I to follow, lass; it calls me not in vain!
Yea, I would join the chorus. Lo! the highway is before
   us,—
   *But what if she, my first beloved, should call to me
   again?*

The wander lure is part o' me, and love is in the heart o'
   me,
   And I would tread the road with you that leads beyond
   the door.
I hear the cry o' laughter, and my feet would follow after,—
   *But what if she, my first beloved, should call to me once
   more?*

Yea, I will follow you, my lass, around the world and
   through, my lass,

To seek the peace o' summer moons that waits beside the
    sea.
We'll leave the past behind us; come, the joy o' life will
    find us,—
*But what if she, my first beloved, should call again to
    me?*

Kendall Banning

Comrades of the Trail

UNTIL the day the world shall die
We shall be comrades, you and I.

For we have seen the morning break
In golden beauty on that lake
That rests in intimate grace before
Our cedar cabin's unlatched door;
And we have heard the rain at night
And blessed our driftwood hearthfire light;
Wakened by thunder, we have crept
Closer and turned again and slept
While the trees crashed, weakening,
And blocked our trail up to the spring.

Dangers of cities never draw
Two close as does the forest's awe;
Beauties of cities never bind
Memory and heart and soul and mind
As does the dawn in forest places,
Or tree-rent moonlight on our faces.

Husband and wife! If that were all!
Not vows alone have made us thrall,

But none can evermore walk free
Bound to each other as are we,
By sky and water, fern and tree.
Mary Carolyn Davies

The Vagrant

I WILL leave the dust of the city street and the noise of the busy town
For the windy moor and the high hill and the peat-stream flowing brown;
I will keep my watch by the camp-fires where the white cliffs lean to the sea,
And dawn shall wake me with golden hands and the rain shall walk with me.

I will seek the place where gypsies roam and strange, wild songs are sung;
I will find once more the magic paths I knew when earth was young,
And the stars will give me comradeship and the wind will be my friend,
And I will send you the fairy gold that lies at the rainbow's end.

Stretch not your hands nor bid me stay, I hear the white road's call,
The sun hath kissed the buds from sleep, and I am one with them all;
But I will send you a golden cloak and a pair of silver shoon,
And a dream that the fairies spin from stars on the other side of the moon.

Pauline Slender

The Gipsy Wedding

ONCE more the gipsy aster
  Her flaunting kerchief waves,
Once more along the wood-ways
His nuts the squirrel saves;
Once more the vagrant passion
Stirs heart of man and maid,
Once more it is October,
Once more the spell is laid.

And to Saint Bartel's altar
Two come where was but one,
With goldenrod and beechleaf
Beneath the amber sun;
Two come, Saint Bartelmeo,
With sunbrowned hand in hand,
To pray your blessing, Father,
Upon the golden band.

There in the tall cathedral
Of tamarack and pine,
The old saint gives the blessing,
The sunbrowned fingers twine.
And down the dusky wood-ways
The gipsy lad and maid
Go hand in hand together
Forever unafraid.

Sara Hamilton Birchall

The Vagabond At Home

OH, it's spring once more in France, and it's spring
in gay Algiers,

And it's spring along the happy Appian Way;
There are cherries in Japan, and the thrushes' joy and tears
　Pipe for England, "There is nowhere such a day!"

How the call rings clear, commanding: "Hurry over, sail afar
　To the date-tree and the banyan's dim domain;
To the Yangtze and the Yalu, where the bell-topped temples are;
　And remember there are castles left in Spain!"

But I hear a whisper steady, blowing down my own home-stream
　Full of all the glad romance I used to know:
　　"Leave the lands beyond to others;
　　Our wee woodfolk are your brothers;
　And the earth is bursting treasure!" So I go.

When the wander urge is on me, there are never bonds that hold;
　When the summons comes, it never comes in vain;
But the foreign trails are either far too new or far too old—
　Give me April in my native woods again!
　　　　　　　　　Ruth Wright Kauffman

The Gipsy Trail

THE white moth to the closing vine,
　The bee to the open clover,
And the gipsy blood to the gipsy blood
　Ever the wide world over.

Ever the wide world over, lass,
　Ever the trail held true,

Over the world and under the world,
   And back at the last to you.

Out of the dark of the gorgio camp,
   Out of the grime and the gray
(Morning waits at the end of the world),
   Gipsy, come away!

The wild boar to the sun-dried swamp,
   The red crane to her reed,
And the Romany lass to the Romany lad
   By the tie of a roving breed.

Morning waits at the end of the world
   Where winds unhaltered play,
Nipping the flanks of their plunging ranks,
   Till the white sea-horses neigh.

The pied snake to the rifted rock,
   The buck to the stony plain,
And the Romany lass to the Romany lad,
   And both to the road again.

Both to the road again, again!
   Out on a clean sea-track—
Follow the cross of the gipsy trail
   Over the world and back!

Follow the Romany patteran
   North where the blue bergs sail,
And the bows are gray with the frozen spray,
   And the masts are shod with mail.

Follow the Romany patteran
   Sheer to the Austral Light,

Where the besom of God is the wild south wind,
  Sweeping the sea-floors white.

Follow the Romany patteran
  West to the sinking sun,
Till the junk-sails lift through the houseless drift,
  And the east and the west are one.

Follow the Romany patteran
  East where the silence broods
By a purple wave on an opal beach
  In the hush of the Mahim Woods.

The wild hawk to the wind-swept sky,
  The deer to the wholesome wold,
And the heart of a man to the heart of a maid,
  As it was in the days of old.

The heart of a man to the heart of a maid—
  Light of my tents, be fleet!
Morning waits at the end of the world,
  And the world is all at our feet!

Rudyard Kipling

St. Bartholomew's On The Hill

BARTHOLOMEW, my brother,
  I like your roomy church;
I like your way of leaving
  No sinners in the lurch.

I wish the world were wealthy
  In ministers like you,

When at the lovely August
You give the blessed dew.

I love your rambling Abbey,
So long ago begun,
Whose choirs are in the tree-tops,
Whose censor is the sun.

Its windows are the morning;
Its rafters are the stars;
The fog-banks float like incense
Up from its purple floors.

And where the ruddy apples
Make lamps in the green gloom,
The flowers in congregation
Are never pressed for room;

But in your hillside chapel,
Gay with its gorgeous paints,
They bow before the Presence,—
Sweet, merry little saints.

Bliss Carman

Fishing

"MEN will grow weary," said the Lord,
"Of working for their bed and board.
They'll weary of the money chase
And want to find a resting place
Where hum of wheel is never heard
And no one speaks an angry word.

And selfishness and greed and pride
And petty motives don't abide.
They'll need a place where they can go
To wash their souls as white as snow.
They will be better men and true
If they can play a day or two."

The Lord then made the brooks to flow
And fashioned rivers here below,
And many lakes; for water seems
Best suited for a mortal's dreams.
He placed about them willow trees
To catch the murmur of the breeze.
And the birds that sing the best
Among the foliage to nest.
He filled each pond and stream and lake
With fish for man to come and take.
Then stretched a velvet carpet deep
On which a weary soul could sleep.

It seemed to me the Good Lord knew
That man would want something to do
When, worn and wearied with the stress
Of battling hard for world success,
When sick at heart of all the strife
And pettiness of daily life.
He knew he'd need, from time to time
To cleanse himself of city grime,
And he would want some place to be
Where hate and greed he'd never see,
And so on lakes and streams and brooks
The Good Lord fashioned fishing nooks.

Edgar A. Guest

A Vagabond Song

THERE is something in the autumn that is native to my blood—
Touch of manner, hint of mood;
And my heart is like a rhyme,
With the yellow and the purple and the crimson keeping time.

The scarlet of the maples can shake me like a cry
Of bugles going by.
And my lonely spirit thrills
To see the frosty asters like a smoke upon the hills.

There is something in October sets the gypsy blood astir;
We must rise and follow her,
When from every hill of flame
She calls and calls each vagabond by name.
Bliss Carman

Have You?

HAVE you ever built a camp-fire at the closing of the day?
  Have you sat and watched the embers glowing red?
With your scanty supper finished and the things all cleared away,
  Have you sat and smoked and thought about your bed?
Of the bed you left behind you in the dwelling-place of man,
  In the much o'er-furnished room you knew of yore;
Ere you sought the silent places where a fellow learns he can
  Do a lot of things he never did before?

Have you ever spread a blanket down beneath the star-
    strewn skies?
  Rolled yourself within its cozy folds to sleep,
At the base of mighty mountains, with their peaks that rise
    and rise?
  Have you known the age-old silence that they keep?
Have you seen the red sun climbing up the eastern slope?
    Then know
  You will ne'er forget those rugged, happy days.
What! You've never known the glory of the new-born day?
    Then go—
  It's a road that's hard to travel—but it pays.

Harry M. Dean

Gypsy-Heart

THE April world is misted with emerald and gold;
  The meadow-larks are calling sweet and keen;
Gypsy-heart is up and off for woodland and for wold,
  Roaming, roaming, roaming through the green.
      Gypsy-heart, away!
    Oh, the wind—the wind and the sun!
  Take the blithe adventure of the fugitive to-day;
    Youth will soon be done.

From buds that May is kissing there trembles forth a soul;
  The rosy boughs are whispering the white;
Gypsy-heart is heedless now of thrush and oriole,
  Dreaming, dreaming, dreaming of delight.
      Gypsy-heart, beware!
    Oh, the song—the song in the blood!
  Magic walks the forest; there's bewitchment on the air.
    Spring is at the flood.

The wings of June are woven of fragrance and of fire;
  Heap roses, crimson roses, for her throne.
Gypsy-heart is anguished with tumultuous desire,
  Seeking, seeking, seeking for its own.
      Gypsy-heart, abide!
    Oh, the far—the far is the near!
  'Tis a foolish fable that the universe is wide.
    All the world is here.

Katharine Lee Bates

A More Ancient Mariner

THE swarthy bee is a buccaneer,
  A burly velveted rover,
Who loves the booming wind in his ear
As he sails the seas of clover.

A waif of the goblin pirate crew,
With not a soul to deplore him,
He steers for the open verge of blue
With the filmy world before him.

. . . .

He harries the ports of the Hollyhocks,
And levies on poor Sweetbrier;
He drinks the whitest wine of Phlox,
And the Rose is his desire.

He hangs in the Willows a night and a day;
He rifles the Buckwheat patches;
Then battens his store of pelf galore
Under the tautest hatches.

He woos the Poppy and weds the Peach,
Inveigles Daffodilly,
And then like a tramp abandons each
For the gorgeous Canada Lily.

. . . .

He dares to boast, along the coast,
The beauty of Highland Heather,—
How he and she, with night on the sea,
Lay out on the hills together.

He pilfers from every port of the wind,
From April to golden autumn;
But the thieving ways of his mortal days
Are those his mother taught him.

. . . .

He never could box the compass round;
He doesn't know port from starboard;
But he knows the gates of the Sundown Straits,
Where the choicest goods are harbored.

He never could see the Rule of Three,
But he knows a rule of thumb
Better than Euclid's, better than yours,
Or the teachers' yet to come.

. . . .

He drones along with his rough sea-song
And the throat of a salty tar,
This devil-may-care, till he makes his lair
By the light of a yellow star.

He looks like a gentleman, lives like a lord,
And works like a Trojan hero;
Then loafs all winter upon his hoard,
With the mercury at zero.

Bliss Carman

Vagabonds

UPON us vagabonds who take
   Our packs and paddles Sunday
The good folk look austerely down,
Though they may smile on Monday.

Some call us pagans, others tramps;
The truth they never knew—
We faithfully attend the Church
Of Saint Bartholomew.

Among the birches on the hill
His holydays are kept
Where thrushes flute the anthems, and
Crumb-charity accept.

The sermon never wearies us;
We hold the Amen pew,
And pay our pew-rent to the Church
Of Saint Bartholomew.

Sara Hamilton Birchall

The Gypsying

I WISH we might go gypsying one day while we're young—
On a blue October morning
Beneath a cloudless sky,
When all the world's a vibrant harp
The winds o' God have strung,
And gay as tossing torches the maples light us by;
The rising sun before us—a golden bubble swung—
I wish we might go gypsying one day while we're young.

I wish we might go gypsying one day before we're old—
To step it with the wild west wind
And sing the while we go,
Through far forgotten orchards
Hung with jewels red and gold;
Through cool and fragrant forests where never sun may
    show,
To stand upon a high hill and watch the mist unfold—
I wish we might go gypsying one day before we're old.

I wish we might go gypsying, dear lad, the while we care.
The while we've heart for hazarding,
The while we've will to sing,
The while we've wit to hear the call
And youth and mirth to spare,
Before a day may find us too sad for gypsying,
Before a day may find us too dull to dream and dare—
I wish we might go gypsying, dear lad, the while we care.
Theodosia Garrison

The Mendicants

WE are as mendicants who wait
    Along the roadside in the sun.
Tatters of yesterday and shreds
Of morrow clothe us every one.

And some are dotards, who believe
And glory in the days of old;
While some are dreamers, harping still
Upon an unknown age of gold.

Hopeless or witless! Not one heeds,
As lavish Time comes down the way

And tosses in the suppliant hat
One great new-minted gold To-day.

. . . .

O foolish ones, put by your care!
Where wants are many, joys are few;
And at the wilding springs of peace,
God keeps an open house for you.

. . . .

But there be others, happier few,
The vagabondish sons of God,
Who know the by-ways and the flowers,
And care not how the world may plod.

They idle down the traffic lands,
And loiter through the woods with spring;
To them the glory of the earth
Is but to hear a bluebird sing.

. . . .

One I remember kept his coin,
And laughing flipped it in the air;
But when two strolling pipe-players
Came by, he tossed it to the pair.

Spendthrift of joy, his childish heart
Danced to their wild outlandish bars;
Then supperless he laid him down
That night, and slept beneath the stars.

Bliss Carman

The Beloved Vagabond

YOU who were once so careless, I can recall you now,
Your blue-gray visionary eyes, your great and open brow,

With naught to bind your heart-strings, and all the world in fee,
You went where all the roads lead, beyond the farthest sea.

Lover of space and skyline, what vision seared your eyes?
What gypsy word was winged to you that bade you gird and rise?
What thread of smoke sent onward your restless, eager feet?
What vagrant heart was waiting your wayward heart to greet?

We, who are kin to the city, across the candles praise
Your tales of camps in twilight, your great and gallant ways,
Your knowledge of the mysteries deep-hidden by the wood,
The pagan trust you placed in man, the world you found so good.

Then leave a *patrin* for mine eyes that I may follow too,
Some day when all the world grows dim, and I shall beckon you;
Across the distant moorland, from beacon furze piled high,
May I, the newest rover, see your fire against the sky!

W. G. Tinckom-Fernandez

The Secret Voices

HAVE you heard the secret voices go whispering in your blood,
Of burning wood and falling leaf and swelling Springtime flood?
Have you felt the tang of lusty wind, the stinging lash of rain,

As tides of Spring march down the days with summer in
  their train?

Have you known the zest and sparkle, felt the magic in
  the air,
And set your feet upon the road that leads to Anywhere?
And seen the skirts of storm-clouds trailing over budding
  trees,
And drunk the wine of virile life down to the very lees?

Have you heard and have you known the voices of the wind,
That bid a man rise up and go and follow till he find
The pot of gold at the rainbow's base,
Or a secret dream in a hidden place. . . .
Have you heard the secret voices whispering that Spring
  has come,
Calling you to rise and follow till you walk into the sun?
Ethel Mannin

The Pool

COME with me, follow me, swift as a moth,
  Ere the wood-doves waken.
Lift the long leaves and look down, look down
Where the light is shaken,
Amber and brown
On the woven ivory roots of the reed,
On a floating flower and a weft of weed
And a feather of froth.

Here in the night all wonders are,
Lapped in the lift of the ripple's swing,—
A silver shell and a shaken star,
And a white moth's wing.
Here the young moon when the mists unclose
Swims like the bud of a golden rose.

I would live like an elf where the wild grapes cling,
I would chase the thrush
From the red rose-berries.
All the day long I would laugh and swing
With the black choke-cherries.

I would shake the bees from the milkweed blooms,
And cool, O cool,
Night after night I would leap in the pool,
And sleep with the fish in the roots of the rush.
Clear, O clear my dreams should be
As the dark, sweet water enfolding me
Safe as a blind shell under the sea.

Marjorie Pickthall

The Turn of the Seasons

A Song of Early Autumn

WHEN late in summer the streams run yellow,
   Burst the bridges and spread into bays;
When berries are black and peaches are mellow,
   And hills are hidden by rainy haze;

When the goldenrod is golden still,
   But the heart of the sunflower is darker and sadder;
When the corn is in stacks on the slope of the hill,
   And slides o'er the path and the striped adder;

When butterflies flutter from clover to thicket,
   Or wave their wings on the drooping leaf;
When the breeze comes shrill with the call of the cricket,
   Grasshoppers' rasp, and rustle of sheaf;

When high in the field the fern-leaves wrinkle,
   And brown is the grass where the mowers have mown;
When low in the meadow the cow-bells tinkle,
   And small brooks crinkle o'er stock and stone.

When heavy and hollow the robin's whistle
   And shadows are deep in the heat of noon;
When the air is white with the down o' the thistle,
   And the sky is red with the harvest moon;

O, Then be chary, young Robert and Mary,
   No time let slip, not a moment wait!
     If the fiddle would play it must stop its tuning,
       And they who would wed must be done with their mooning;
So, let the churn rattle, see well to the cattle,
   And pile the wood by the barn-yard gate!

Richard Watson Gilder

Old Age

I HAVE heard the wild geese,
   I have seen the leaves fall,
There was frost last night
On the garden wall.
It is gone to-day
And I hear the wind call.
The wind? . . . That is all.

If the swallow will light
When the evening is near;
If the crane will not scream
Like a soul in fear;
I will think no more
Of the dying year.
And the wind, its seer.

Cale Young Rice

Turn O' The Year

THIS is the time when bit by bit
  The days begin to lengthen sweet
And every minute gained is joy—
And love stirs in the heart of a boy.

This is the time the sun, of late
Content to lie abed till eight,
Lifts up betimes his sleepy head—
And love stirs in the heart of a maid.

This is the time we dock the night
Of a whole hour of candlelight;
When song of linnet and thrush is heard—
And love stirs in the heart of a bird.

This is the time when sword-blades green,
With gold and purple damascene,
Pierce the brown crocus-bed a-row—
And love stirs in a heart I know.

Katharine Tynan

April Music

THE lyric sound of laughter
  Fills all the April hills,
The joy-song of the crocus,
  The mirth of daffodils.

They ring their golden changes
  Through all the azure vales;
The sunny cowslips answer,
  Athwart the reedy swales.

Far down the woodland aisleways
  The trillium's voice is heard;
The little wavering wind-flowers
  Join in with jocund word.

The white cry of the dogwood
  Mounts up against the sky;
The breath of violet music
  Upon the breeze goes by.

Give me to hear, O April,
  These choristers of thine
Calling across the distance
  Serene and hyaline;

To clear my clouded vision
  Bedimmed and dulled so long,
And heal my aching spirit
  With fragrance that is song!
                              Clinton Scollard

The Year's Awakening

HOW do you know that the pilgrim track
  Along the belting zodiac
Swept by the sun in his seeming rounds
Is traced by now to the Fishes' bounds
And into the Ram, when weeks of cloud
Have wrapt the sky in a clammy shroud,
And never as yet a tinct of spring
Has shown in the Earth's apparelling;
  Oh, vespering bird, how do you know,
    How do you know?

How do you know, deep underground,
Hid in your bed from sight and sound,
Without a turn in temperature,
With weather life can scarce endure,
That light has won a fraction's strength,
And day put on some moments' length,
Whereof in merest rote will come,
Weeks hence, mild airs that do not numb;
  Oh, crocus root, how do you know,
    How do you know?

Thomas Hardy

Spring's Answer

I HEARD God calling
  And I came,
His Sun signalled me
With its flame.
His Wind called me
With its song.
His Birds said they had been waiting
Over long.
His little Brooks ran tumbling
Down the hills,
Luring me with laughter
Of rocky rills.
His Grasses, yellow-green,
Standing in the sun,
Held up their fingers
For me to come.
Heart of Oak and heart of Pine
Beat a faint tattoo—
Flowing sap in bole and bud

Climbing up anew.
Till at last the summons
Set my heart aflame—
I heard God calling,
And I came!

Edwin Osgood Grover

Morning Song

THE grass is taller, greener,
   And the birds more loud;
The flowers open freshly
   To a sky of cloud.

And man awakens gladly
   In a world that's good,
And thrills to some new beauty
   Not quite understood.

Though all the world is clouded
   It's a gray delight—
For spring is swelling, swelling,
   And it rained last night.

Lancaster Pollard

April Weather

SOON, ah, soon the April weather
   With the sunshine at the door,
And the mellow melting rain-wind
   Sweeping from the South once more.

Soon the rosy maples budding,
  And the willows putting forth,
Misty crimson and soft yellow
  In the valleys of the North.

Soon the hazy purple distance,
  Where the cabined heart takes wing,
Eager for the old migration
  In the magic of the spring.

Soon, ah, soon the budding windflowers
  Through the forest white and frail,
And the odorous wild cherry
  Gleaming in her ghostly veil.

Soon, about the waking uplands
  The hepaticas in blue,—
Children of the first warm sunlight
  In their sober Quaker hue,—

All our shining little sisters
  Of the forest and the field,
Lifting up their quiet faces
  With the secret half revealed.

Soon across the folding twilight
  Of the round earth hushed to hear,
The first robin at his vespers
  Calling far, serene and clear.

Soon the waking and the summons,
  Starting sap in bole and blade,
And the bubbling marshy whisper
  Seeping up through bog and glade.

Soon the frogs in silver chorus
  Through the night, from marsh and swale,
Blowing in their tiny oboes
  All the joy that shall not fail,—

Passing up the old earth rapture
  By a thousand streams and rills,
From the red Virginian valleys
  To the blue Canadian hills.

Soon, ah, soon the splendid impulse,
  Nomad longing, vagrant whim,
When a man's false angels vanish
  And the truth comes back to him.

Soon the majesty, the vision,
  And the old unfaltering dream,
Faith to follow, strength to stablish,
  Will to venture and to seem;

All the radiance, the glamour,
  The expectancy and poise,
Of this ancient life renewing
  Its temerities and joys.

Soon the immemorial magic
  Of the young Aprilian moon,
And the wonder of thy friendship
  In the twilight—soon, ah, soon!
                    Bliss Carman

The Runaway

WHAT are you doing, little day-moon,
  Over the April hill?

What are you doing, up so soon,
Climbing the sky with silver shoon?
What are you doing at half-past noon,
   Slipping along so still?

Are you so eager, the heights unwon,
   That you cannot wait,
But, unheeding of wind and sun,
Out of your nest of night must run,
Up where the day is far from done,
   Shy little shadow-mate?

Up and away then—with young mists
   Tripping, along the blue!
Dance and dally and promise trysts
Unto each that around you lists;
For, little moon, not a one but wists
   April's the time to woo!

Cale Young Rice

Spring Market

IT'S foolish to bring money
   To any spring wood,
Jewels won't help you,
   Gold's no good.

Silver won't buy you
   One small leaf.
You may bring joy here,
   You may bring grief.

You should look for
 Tufted moss,
Marked where a light foot
 Ran across.

Where the old rose hips
 Shrivel brown
And dried clematis
 Bloom hangs down.

There you'll find what
 Everyman needs,
Wild religion
 Without any creeds,

Green that lifts its
 Blossoming head,
New life springing
 Among the dead.

You needn't bring money
 To this market place,
Or think you can bargain for
 Wild flower grace.

Louise Driscoll

Song in March

I SING the first green leaf upon the bough,
 The tiny kindling flame of emerald fire,
The stir amid the roots of reeds, and how
 The sap will flush the briar.

I sing the sweeping beryl on the slopes,
   Ephemeræ that come before the bees,
The ferns renascent, and the virgin hopes
   Of pale anemones.

I sing the dream's unfolding, and I sing
   The chrysalis broken by the ice-freed shore,
The clear air winnowed by the bluebird's wing,
   And April at the door!

Clinton Scollard

Flower Chorus

O SUCH a commotion under the ground,
   When March called "Ho, there! ho!"
Such spreading of rootlets far and wide,
   Such whisperings to and fro!
"Are you ready?" the Snowdrop asked,
   "'Tis time to start, you know."
"Almost, my dear!" the Scilla replied,
   "I'll follow as soon as you go."
Then "Ha! ha! ha!" a chorus came
   Of laughter sweet and low,
From millions of flowers under the ground,
   Yes, millions beginning to grow.

"I'll promise my blossoms," the Crocus said,
   "When I hear the blackbird sing."
And straight thereafter Narcissus cried,
   "My silver and gold I'll bring."
"And ere they are dulled," another spoke,
   "The hyacinth bells shall ring."
But the Violet only murmured "I'm here,"

And sweet grew the air of spring.
Then "Ha! ha! ha!" a chorus came
　Of laughter sweet and low,
From millions of flowers under the ground,
　Yes, millions beginning to grow.

Oh, the pretty brave things, thro' the coldest days
　Imprisoned in walls of brown,
They never lost heart tho' the blast shrieked loud,
　And the sleet and the hail came down;
But patiently each wrought her wonderful dress,
　Or fashioned her beautiful crown,
And now they are coming to lighten the world
　Still shadowed by winter's frown.
And well may they cheerily laugh "Ha! ha!"
　In laughter sweet and low,
The millions of flowers under the ground,
　Yes, millions beginning to grow.
Ralph Waldo Emerson

April's Coming

APRIL comes with sudden showers,
　Chilling winds and sunny hours.
April comes with growing green
On the trees still winter-lean.
April brings the singing bird
And a joy that is absurd.
April comes and April goes,
But the flowers April sows—
Earth's obituary tears—
Wake the immemorial years.
So with Spring's passing comes

Summer with her borrowed drums;
Fall and winter in a ring
Till April comes again with spring.

Lancaster Pollard

The Secret

ON that first day so singular
   Under the ground,
It was too dark for crescent or for star,
Too deep for sound.

And lying there one thought alone
I could not still:
How soon would snow-white cherry buds be blown
Across the hill.

And then a voice within the tomb
Said very low:
"When April lights her first sharp flame of bloom
You'll know!"

John Richard Moreland

Spring

ALL the lanes are lyric,
   All the bushes sing;
You are at your kissing,
     Spring!

Romping with your children
  Do not fail to bring
Mary to the haystack,
    Spring!

Froth upon the fingers,
  Bosom for a king,
Speed her from the milking,
    Spring!

Norman Gale

April Weather

OH, hush, my heart, and take thine ease,
  For here is April weather!
The daffodils beneath the trees
  Are all a-row together.

The thrush is back with his old note;
  The scarlet tulip blowing;
And white, aye, white as my love's throat—
  The dogwood boughs are growing.

The lilac bush is sweet again;
  Down every wind that passes,
Fly flakes from hedgerow and from lane;
  The bees are in the grasses.

And Grief goes out, and Joy comes in,
  And care is but a feather;
And every lad his love can win,
  For here is April weather.

Lizette Woodworth Reese

Renewal

APRIL, when I heard
  Your lyrical low word,
And when upon the hawthorn hedge your first white blossom
    stirred,

Something strangely came—
Something I cannot name—
And touched my heart, and cleansed my soul with a re-
    viving flame.

When the yellow gleam
Of your hosts that stream—
Jonquil, buttercup, and crocus—made the world a goiden
    dream,

Something, April, said
To my heart that bled—
Bled with old remembrance—"Lo, the grief-strewn days
    are fled!"

Sursum corda! Now,
When blooms the apple-bough,
April, of your pity, let your light rain kiss my brow;

Heal me, if you will;
Bathe my heart until
I am one with your first primrose or the shining daffodil!
Charles Hanson Towne

April

SOMETHING tapped at my window pane,
  Someone called me without my door.
Someone laughed like the tinkle o' rain,
The robin echoed it o'er and o'er.

I threw the door and the window wide;
Sun and the touch of the breeze and then—
"Ah, were you expecting me, dear?" she cried,
And here was April come back again.
Theodosia Garrison

The Immortal

SPRING has come up from the South again,
With soft mists in her hair,
And a warm wind in her mouth again,
And budding everywhere.
Spring has come up from the South again,
And her skies are azure fire,
And around her is the awakening
  Of all the world's desire.

Spring has come up from the South again,
And dreams are in her eyes,
And music is in her mouth again
Of love, the never-wise.
Spring has come up from the South again,
And bird and flower and bee
Know that she is their life and joy—
  And immortality!

Cale Young Rice

Spring

I SAID in my heart, "I am sick of four walls and a ceiling.
I have need of the sky.
I have business with the grass.

I will up and get me away where the hawk is wheeling,
Lone and high,
And the slow clouds go by.
I will get me away to the waters that glass
The clouds as they pass,
To the waters that lie
Like the heart of a maiden aware of a doom drawing nigh
And dumb for sorcery of impending joy.
I will get me away to the woods.
Spring, like a huntsman's boy,
Halloos along the hillsides and unhoods
The falcon in my will.
The dogwood calls me, and the sudden thrill
That breaks in apple blooms down country roads
Plucks me by the sleeve and nudges me away.
The sap is in the boles today,
And in my veins a pulse that yearns and goads."

When I got to the woods, I found out
What the Spring was about,
With her gypsy ways,
And her heart ablaze,
Coming up from the South
With the wander-lure of witch songs in her mouth.
For the sky
Stirred and grew soft and swimming as a lover's eye
As she went by;
The air
Made love to all it touched, as if its care
Were all to spare;
The earth
Prickled with lust of birth;
The woodland streams
Babbled the incoherence of the thousand dreams
Wherewith the warm sun teems.

And out of the frieze
Of the chestnut trees
I heard
The sky and the fields and the thickets find voice in a bird.
The goldenwing—hark!
How he drives his song
Like a golden nail
Through the hush of the air!
I thrill to his cry in the leafage there;
I respond to the new life mounting under the bark.
I shall not be long
To follow
With eft and bulrush, bee and bud and swallow,
On the old trail.

.   .   .   .

Spring in the world!
And all things are made new!
There was never a mote that whirled
In the nebular morn,
There was never a brook that purled
Where the hills were born,
There was never a leaf uncurled—
Not the first that grew—
Nor a bee-flight hurled,
Nor a bird-note skirled,
Nor a cloud-wisp swirled
In the depth of the blue,
More alive and afresh and impromptu, more thoughtless and certain and free,
More a-shout with the glee
Of the Unknown new-burst on the wonder, than here, than here,
In the re-wrought sphere
Of the new-born year—
Now, now,

When the greenlet sings on the red-bud bough
Where the blossoms are whispering "I and thou"—"I and
    thou,"
And a lass at the turn looks after a lad with a dawn on her
    brow,
And the world is just made—now!

Spring in the heart!
With her pinks and pearls and yellows!
Spring, fellows,
And we too feel the little green leaves a-start
Across the bare-twigged winter of the mart.
The campus is reborn in us today;
The old grip stirs our hearts with new-old joy;
Again bursts bonds for madcap holiday
The eternal boy.

Richard Hovey

Blind

THE Spring blew trumpets of color;
   Her Green sang in my brain—
I heard a blind man groping
   "Tap—tap" with his cane;

I pitied him in his blindness;
   But can I boast, "I see"?
Perhaps there walks a spirit
   Close by, who pities me,—

A spirit who hears me tapping
   The five-sensed cane of mind
Amid such unguessed glories—
   That I am worse than blind.

Harry Kemp

Spring Song

MAKE me over, mother April,
  When the sap begins to stir!
When thy flowery hand delivers
All the mountain-prisoned rivers,
And thy great heart beats and quivers
To revive the days that were,
Make me over, mother April,
When the sap begins to stir!

Take my dust and all my dreaming,
Count my heart-beats one by one,
Send them where the winters perish;
Then some golden noon re-cherish
And restore them in the sun,
Flower and scent and dust and dreaming,
With their heart-beats every one.

Set me in the urge and tide-drift
Of the streaming hosts a-wing!
Breast of scarlet, throat of yellow,
Raucous challenge, wooings mellow—
Every migrant is my fellow,
Making northward with the spring.
Loose me in the urge and tide-drift
Of the streaming hosts a-wing!

Shrilling pipe or fluting whistle,
In the valleys come again;
Fife of frog and call of tree-toad,
All my brothers, five or three-toed,
With their revel no more vetoed,
Making music in the rain,

Shrilling pipe or fluting whistle,
In the valleys come again.

Make me of thy seed to-morrow,
When the sap begins to stir!
Tawny light-foot, sleepy bruin,
Bright-eyes in the orchard ruin,
Gnarl the good life goes askew in,
Whisky-jack or tanager,—
Make me anything to-morrow,
When the sap begins to stir!

Make me even (How do I know?)
Like my friend the gargoyle there;
It may be the heart within him
Swells that doltish hands should pin him
Fixed forever in mid-air.
Make me even sport for swallows,
Like the soaring gargoyle there!

Give me the old clue to follow,
Through the labyrinth of night!
Clod of clay with heart of fire,
Things that burrow and aspire,
With the vanishing desire,
For the perishing delight,—
Only the old clue to follow,
Through the labyrinth of night!

Make me over, mother April,
When the sap begins to stir!
Fashion me from swamp or meadow,
Garden plot or ferny shadow,
Hyacinth or humble burr!
Make me over, mother April,
When the sap begins to stir!

Let me hear the far, low summons,
When the silver winds return;
Rills that run and streams that stammer,
Goldenwing with his loud hammer,
Icy brooks that brawl and clamor,
Where the Indian willows burn;
Let me hearken to the calling,
When the silver winds return,

Till recurring and recurring,
Long since wandered and come back,
Like a whim of Grieg's or Gounod's,
This same self, bird, bud, or Bluenose,
Some day I may capture (Who knows?)
Just the one last joy I lack,
Waking to the far new summons,
When the old spring winds come back.

For I have no choice of being,
When the sap begins to climb,—
Strong insistence, sweet intrusion,
Vasts and verges of illusion,—
So I win, to time's confusion,
The one perfect pearl of time,
Joy and joy and joy forever,
Till the sap forgets to climb!

Make me over in the morning
From the rag-bag of the world!
Scraps of dream and duds of daring,
Home-brought stuff from far sea-faring,
Faded colors once so flaring,
Shreds of banners long since furled!
Hues of ash and glints of glory,
In the rag-bag of the world!

Let me taste the old immortal
Indolence of life once more;
Not recalling or foreseeing,
Let the great slow joys of being
Well my heart through as of yore!
Let me taste the old immortal
Indolence of life once more!

Give me the old drink for rapture,
The delirium to drain!
All my fellows drank in plenty
At the Three-Score Inns and Twenty
From the mountains to the main!
Give me the old drink for rapture,
The delirium to drain!

Only make me over, April
When the sap begins to stir!
Make me man or make me woman,
Make me oaf or ape or human,
Cup of flower or cone of fir;
Make me anything but neuter
When the sap begins to stir!

Bliss Carman

The Sweet, Low Speech Of The Rain

IT is pleasant to lie in the gloaming
  When the autumn is on the wane,
And the careful, rejoicing reaper
  Has gathered and stored his grain,

And hear at the doors and the windows
  The sweet, low speech of the rain.

To put by the thought of the sailor
  Far out on the storm-rocked main,
Where the fierce waves leap and struggle.
  Like beasts in passionate pain,
And lie by the hearth and listen
  To the sweet, low speech of the rain.

Ah, May has the burst of the blossom,
  And the red of the willow vein,
And the glad uplift of the flowers
  That lead in the fragrant train;
But nothing so dear as the sweet, low
  Speech of the autumn rain.

July has the rose and the purple,
  And the sunset's golden stain
On the river that draws thro' the valley
  A glittering, wave-linked chain;
But never this lyrical, tremulous,
  Sweet, low speech of the rain.

Each heart knows the joy of the winter,
  The drift of the snow on the plain,
The book and the charm of the fireside,
  The icicles fringing the pane;
But ah, for the faltering, pausing,
  Sweet, low speech of the rain.

Old friends of my heart come to-morrow,
  Remembrance, Regret, and Pain,
But to-night I will lie in the gloaming
  And be lulled by the lure of the rain—

And the rhythmical, lyrical, rhyming,
   Sweet, low speech of the rain.
                      Ella Higginson

Early Spring

ONCE more the Heavenly Power
   Makes all things new,
And domes the red-plowed hills
   With loving blue;
The blackbirds have their wills,
   The throstles too.

Opens a door in Heaven;
   From skies of glass
A Jacob's ladder falls
   On greening grass,
And o'er the mountain-walls
   Young angels pass.

Before them fleets the shower,
   And burst the buds,
And shine the level lands,
   And flash the floods;
The stars are from their hands
   Flung through the woods,

The woods with living airs
   How softly fanned,
Light airs from where the deep,
   All down the sand,
Is breathing in his sleep,
   Heard by the land.

O, follow, leaping blood,
  The season's lure!
O heart, look down and up,
  Serene, secure,
Warm as the crocus cup,
  Like snow-drops pure!

Past, Future glimpse and fade
  Through some slight spell,
A gleam from yonder vale,
  Some far blue fell,
And sympathies, how frail,
  In sound and smell!

Till at thy chuckled note,
  Thou twinkling bird,
The fairy fancies range,
  And, lightly stirred,
Ring little bells of change
  From word to word.

For now the Heavenly Power
  Makes all things new,
And thaws the cold, and fills
  The flower with dew;
The blackbirds have their wills,
  The poets too.

Alfred Tennyson

Spring

SPRING, with that nameless pathos in the air
  Which dwells with all things fair,

Spring, with her golden suns and silver rain,
Is with us once again.

Out in the lonely woods the jasmine burns
Its fragrant lamps, and turns
Into a royal court with green festoons
The banks of dark lagoons.

In the deep heart of every forest tree
The blood is all aglee,
And there's a look about the leafless bowers
As if they dreamed of flowers.

Yet still on every side we trace the hand
Of Winter in the land,
Save where the maple reddens on the lawn,
Flushed by the season's dawn;

Or where, like those strange semblances we find
That age to childhood bind,
The elms put on, as if in Nature's scorn,
The brown of Autumn corn.

As yet the turf is dark, although you know
That, not a span below,
A thousand germs are groping through the gloom,
And soon will burst their tomb.

Already, here and there, on frailest stems
Appear some azure gems,
Small as might deck, upon a gala day
The forehead of a fay.

In gardens you may note amid the dearth,
The crocus breaking earth;

And near the snowdrop's tender white and green,
The violet in its screen.

But many gleams and shadows needs must pass
Along the budding grass,
And weeks go by, before the enamored South
Shall kiss the rose's mouth.

Still there's a sense of blossoms yet unborn
In the sweet airs of morn;
One almost looks to see the very street
Grow purple at his feet.

At times a fragrant breeze comes floating by,
And brings, you know not why,
A feeling as when eager crowds await
Before a palace gate

Some wondrous pageant; and you scarce would start,
If from a beech's heart
A blue-eyed Dryad, stepping forth, should say,
"Behold me! I am May!"

Henry Timrod

April, April

APRIL, April,
Laugh thy girlish laughter;
Then, the moment after,
Weep thy girlish tears,
April, that mine ears
Like a lover greetest,

If I tell thee, sweetest,
All my hopes and fears.
April, April,
Laugh thy golden laughter,
But, the moment after,
Weep thy golden tears!
William Watson

April Rain

IT is not raining rain for me,
   It's raining daffodils;
In every dimpled drop I see
   Wild flowers on the hills.

The clouds of gray engulf the day
   And overwhelm the town;
It is not raining rain to me,
   It's raining roses down.

It is not raining rain to me,
   But fields of clover bloom,
Where any buccaneering bee
   Can find a bed and room.

A health unto the happy,
   A fig for him who frets!
It is not raining rain to me,
   It's raining violets.

Robert Loveman

April

AN altered look about the hills;
A Tyrian light the village fills;
A wider sunrise in the dawn;
A deeper twilight on the lawn;
A print of a vermilion foot;
A purple finger on the slope;
A flippant fly upon the pane;
A spider at his trade again;
An added strut in chanticleer;
A flower expected everywhere;
An axe shrill singing in the woods;
Fern-odors on untravelled roads,—
All this, and more I cannot tell,
A furtive look you know as well,
And Nicodemus' mystery
Receives its annual reply.

Emily Dickinson

April Morning

I WOULD spend a morning
With an April apple tree,
Speaking to it softly
  And laughing out in glee.

All the summer sunshine
  And all the winter moon
Are shining in the blossoms
  That will be gone so soon.

I will spend a morning
   With a friendly apple tree,
Hearing many secrets
   That it will tell to me.

I will take a morning
   To drink the beauty in;
I will take a morning—
   But how shall I begin?
George Elliston

May-Lure

HOW the heart pulls at its tether
   In the magic warm spring weather!
How the blood leaps in its courses
When the deep ebullient forces
Break the bosom brown of earth!

   It is worth
All a man can scrape or squander
Just to idle, just to wander
Forth from trade, away from duty,
Revelling in all the beauty
And the glamour of the May.

   Who to-day
Cares a fig for any other
Thought save this: The earth, great mother,
Has turned kind, has banished gloom and dole;
Music, that audient outlet for the soul,
Comes in, and grief goes out, and life is whole.
Richard Burton

Sunrise

DAY!
    Faster and more fast,
O'er night's brim, day boils at last:
Boils, pure gold, o'er the cloud-cup's brim
Where spurting and suppressed it lay,
For not a froth-flake touched the rim
Of yonder gap in the solid gray
Of the eastern cloud, an hour away;
But forth one wavelet, then another, curled,
Till the whole sunrise, not to be suppressed,
Rose, reddened, and its seething breast
Flickered in bounds, grew gold, then overflowed the world.
                              Robert Browning

The Throstle

"SUMMER is coming, summer is coming,
    I know it, I know it, I know it.
Light again, leaf again, life again, love again,"
    Yes, my wild little Poet.

Sing the new year in under the blue.
    Last year you sang it as gladly.
"New, new, new, new!" Is it then *so* new
    That you should carol so madly?

"Love again, song again, nest again, young again,"
    Never a prophet so crazy!
And hardly a daisy as yet, little friend,
    See, there is hardly a daisy.

"Here again, here, here, here, happy year!"
  Oh, warble unchidden, unbidden!
Summer is coming, is coming, my dear,
  And all the winters are hidden.
Alfred Tennyson

Tell All The World

TELL all the world that summer's here again
  With song and joy; tell them, that they may know
How, on the hillside, in the shining fields
  New clumps of violets and daisies grow.

Tell all the world that summer's here again,
  That white clouds voyage through a sky so still
With blue tranquillity, it seems to hang
  One windless tapestry, from hill to hill.

Tell all the world that summer's here again:
  Folk go about so solemnly and slow,
Walking each one his grooved and ordered way—
  I fear that, otherwise, they will not know!
Harry Kemp

Sorrow in a Garden

HERE to this ancient garden
  When wintry days had flown
I came, with Comrade Sorrow
  To dwell with her alone.

Within this sweet seclusion
    Far from the world's rude stare
What exquisite communings
    Sorrow and I would share!

What banquets of remembrance,
    What luxury of tears
With Sorrow in a garden
    Through the rose scented years!

But one day when she called me
    I did not hear her voice;
I only heard the lilies
    Which sang, Rejoice! Rejoice!

For *June* was in the garden
    And June was in my heart,—
I had forgot pale Sorrow
    And now we dwell apart.

But often in the twilight
    When birds and gardens sleep
I feel her presence with me
    Her arms about me creep.

And when the ghost of Summer
    With the dead roses talks
I hear her softly sobbing
    Along the moon-lit walks.

I never can forget her
    So intimate were we
But when I walk my garden
    She comes no more to me.

                      May Riley Smith

The Naturalist On A June Sunday

MY old gardener leans on his hoe,
Tells me the way that green things grow;
"Goin' to church? Why no.
All nature's church enough for me!"
Says he.

"Preachin' o' flower and choir o' bird,
An' the wind passin' the plate—
Sweetest service that ever I heard,
That's straight!
Eternal Rest?
What for, friend?
Gimme a swarm o' bees to tend,
A honey-makin', world without end,
That's what I'd like the best!
(Scoop 'em right up an' find the queen,
They'd not sting me—the bees ain' mean!)

"Heaven's all right!
But still I guess I'll kinder miss
The Lady Lunar moth at night
And the White Wanderer butterfly
Crawlin' out of its chrysalis!
I want my heaven human too,
'Twixt me an' you—
Why I'd jus' love to see
A chipmunk hop up to the Lord
An' eat right out o' His dread Hand
Same as it does to me!
Eternity—eternity—
Don't it sound grand?
But say

What's the matter with today?
Just step into the wood an' take a look!
Ain't that a page o' teachin' from the Holy Book?
'He that hath eyes to see
An' ears to hear'—
That's good enough for me!
I guess God's pretty near,
He'll understand, I know,
Why I ain't in no hurry to let June go!"

My old gardener turns to his hoe,
Helping the green things how to grow,
"The Missis can go to church for me!
Amen!" says he.

Leonora Speyer

Summer[1]

BY sea and by land,
In the water-wooed marshes or meadows wide-reaching and bland,
The summer is regal and rich, the summer on every hand
Spills largesses splendid to mortals, to women and men.
      For when
Is the breeze sweeter fraught with the breath of the hay,
Is the thrush-note more calm or the robin's loud lay
More blithe, or the rose more the queen of the day?
      Now say,
What month is more bounteous in beauties, in balms,
      In lyrics, in psalms,
In gold-heart fair fancies of sunset, and calms

[1] From "Dumb in June"

Of twilight, or after-glows wondrously clear?
          One may hear
The booming of bees and the brook's lulled refrain,
The stream's liquid epic, the grasshopper's plain,
The frog's bass reiterant languor at night,
The day-long and dark-long sound-woof, interplight
With dreamings and memories somber or bright.

        A very miracle,
     I saw a moment gone:
A honeysuckle, vine and bloom,
    Lustrous green and coral red,
     I glimpsed above my head
Shedding a rapt perfume.
And then this marvel fell
    That I would dwell upon:
A bird—nay, rather say an airy sprite
    Compact of color, light,
And a most ravishing power of flight,
    Darted from nowhere, somewhere,
        And alighted there,
    And sat at gaze a moment or twain,
    And then was off again.
Not Wordsworth's cuckoo were a dearer guest
        Unto my quest,
   So insubstantial, spirit small
   And fleetsome in his call;
       Ah, ye know well
It was the humming-bird whereof I tell.

This mother-month of Summer holds her place
       Not only by the grace
Attending on her many winsome ways,—
       Her flower-gifts, her bird-lays,
       Her bridal form and face,—

But by what went before and cometh after;
   April tears, May blooms and laughter,
   September's blazonry, and then October
Fruit-ripe and hushed and most imperially sober
   With sense of harvest dignity and worth.
      Thus, memory and expectation,
   Spring-gleams, fruitions of the fall,
   Encircle June and give unto her station
A reverend look, a light historical;
Child, maiden, matron, she is each and all.

Richard Burton

Autumn

THE morns are meeker than they were,
   The nuts are getting brown;
The berry's cheek is plumper,
   The rose is out of town.

The maple wears a gayer scarf,
   The field a scarlet gown.
Lest I should be old-fashioned,
   I'll put a trinket on.

Emily Dickinson

Overtones

I HEARD a bird at break of day
   Sing from the autumn trees
A song so mystical and calm,
   So full of certainties,
No man, I think, could listen long

Except upon his knees.
Yet this was but a simple bird,
Alone, among dead trees.
William Alexander Percy

Carouse

AUTUMN, in her scarlet cloak,
Comes tumbling down the hills.
Oh, she is tipsy with her dreams
That the blue day distils;
An amber cup is in her hands
From which the wonder spills.

Now leaf and vine turn golden brown,
And purple asters shine
Along the roads where Autumn runs,
Drunken with mystic wine.
The world is one vast tapestry
Of intricate design.

Where Autumn lurches through the dusk
In raiment wildly red,
A crowd of urchins follow her,
With many a tousled head—
Chrysanthemums, like naughty boys,
Driving the crone to bed!
Charles Hanson Towne

A Song in Autumn

AUTUMN, Autumn, give me of your crimson,
Give it me for courage, for the year has left me meek,
And your crimson banners flying, as the sign of your defying,
Shall dare my heart's denying the patience of the weak.

Autumn, Autumn, give me of your yellow,
  Give it unto me for hope—the hope I could not hold;
For where your gold is burning I feel the dream returning,
  The darling pain of yearning whose passing left me old.

Autumn, Autumn, take me to your heart so,
  The bold heart, the singing heart whose strength shall make me strong;
Send my healed life faring in colors of your wearing,
  Your gold and crimson bearing, against a grief too long.

Theodosia Garrison

An Autumn Garden

MY tent stands in a garden
Of aster and golden-rod,
Tilled by the rain and the sunshine,
And sown by the hand of God,—
An old New England pasture
Abandoned to peace and time,
And by the magic of beauty
Reclaimed to the sublime.

About it are golden woodlands
Of tulip and hickory;
On the open ridge behind it
You may mount to a glimpse of sea,—
The far-off, blue, Homeric
Rim of the world's great shield,
A border of boundless glamour
For the soul's familiar field.

In purple and gray-wrought lichen
The boulders lie in the sun;
Along its grassy footpath
The white-tailed rabbits run.
The crickets work and chirrup
Through the still afternoon;
And the owl calls at twilight
Under the frosty moon.

The odorous wild grape clambers
Over the tumbling wall,
And through the autumnal quiet
The chestnuts open and fall.
Sharing Time's freshness and fragrance,
Part of the earth's great soul,
Here man's spirit may ripen
To wisdom serene and whole.

Shall we not grow with the asters?—
Never reluctant nor sad,
Not counting the cost of being,
Living to dare and be glad.
Shall we not lift with the crickets
A chorus of ready cheer,
Braving the frost of oblivion,
Quick to be happy here?

The deep red cones of the sumach
And the woodbine's crimson sprays
Have bannered the common roadside
For the pageant of passing days.
These are the oracles Nature
Fills with her holy breath,
Giving them glory of color,
Transcending the shadow of death.

Here in the sifted sunlight
A spirit seems to brood
On the beauty and worth of being,
In tranquil, instinctive mood;
And the heart, athrob with gladness
Such as the wise earth knows,
Wells with a full thanksgiving
For the gifts that life bestows:

For the ancient and virile nurture
Of the teeming primordial ground,
For the splendid gospel of color,
The rapt revelations of sound;
For the morning-blue above us
And the rusted gold of the fern,
For the chickadee's call to valor
Bidding the faint-heart turn;

For fire and running water,
Snowfall and summer rain;
For sunsets and quiet meadows,
The fruit and the standing grain;
For the solemn hour of moonrise
Over the crest of trees,
When the mellow lights are kindled
In the lamps of the centuries.

For those who wrought aforetime,
Led by the mystic strain
To strive for the larger freedom,
And live for the greater gain;
For plenty and peace and playtime,
The homely goods of earth,
And for rare immaterial treasures
Accounted of little worth;

For art and learning and friendship,
Where beneficent truth is supreme,
Those everlasting cities
Built on the hills of dream;
For all things growing and goodly
That foster this life, and breed
The immortal flower of wisdom
Out of the mortal seed.

But most of all for the spirit
That cannot rest nor bide
In stale and sterile convenience,
Nor safety proven and tried,
But still inspired and driven,
Must seek what better may be,
And up from the loveliest garden
Must climb for a glimpse of sea.

Bliss Carman

September

THE wind comes up across the hill, the wind goes laughing by.
It's time to put your bonnet on, and let your stitching lie;
It's time to take your basket up, and follow on with me,
Along the road and up the hill, strange countries for to see.

For oh, the fields are golden now, the sun is sweet as wine,
The lake lies blue beneath us, and the leaves are thick and fine;
The fluffy clouds are drifting by, the winds are all a-blow;
The geese are flying south before the vanguards of the snow.

Come out, come out across the hills! The golden blossoms call,
September lifts her trumpet to her lips, and comrades all,
But hearken to the ringing cry she sends from hill to hill—
The scarlet leaves come fluttering down, the asters all are still.

Come out, come out, and leave your seam, and put your spinning by!
The sweet September calls us before the flowers die.
The shimmering hills are free to us, the hours are golden sweet.
Come out, dear love, and find my heart the pathway for your feet!

Sara Hamilton Birchall

Days Like These

I LIKE the tangled brakes and briers,
The hazy smoke of forest fires;

The misty hills' soft robe of brown,
The ravished fields' regretful frown:

The wrinkled road's unconscious snare,
The free, unbreathed and fragrant air.

I like the wide, unworried sky,
The resting wind's contented sigh;

The rustle of the vagrant leaves,
The whisper in the standing sheaves;

The birds' lament for summer lost,
The stinging challenge of the frost.

The sturdy life of stalwart trees
Thrills in my veins on days like these!
Ella Elizabeth Egbert

Indian Summer

THESE are the days when birds come back,
A very few, a bird or two,
To take a backward look.

These are the days when skies put on
The old, old sophistries of June—
A blue and gold mistake.

Oh, fraud that cannot cheat the bee,
Almost thy plausibility
Induces my belief,

Till ranks of seeds their witness bear,
And softly through the altered air
Hurries a timid leaf!

Oh, sacrament of summer days,
Oh, last communion in the haze,
Permit a child to join,

Thy sacred emblems to partake,
Thy consecrated bread to break,
Taste thine immortal wine!
Emily Dickinson

The Deserted Pasture

I LOVE the stony pasture
That no one else will have.
The old gray rocks so friendly seen,
So durable and brave.

In tranquil contemplation
It watches through the year,
Seeing the frosty stars arise,
The slender moons appear.

Its music is the rain-wind,
Its choristers the birds,
And there are secrets in its heart
Too wonderful for words.

It keeps the bright-eyed creatures
That play about its walls,
Though long ago its milking herds
Were banished from their stalls.

Only the children come there,
For buttercups in May,
Or nuts in autumn, where it lies
Dreaming the hours away.

Long since its strength was given
To making good increase,
And now its soul is turned again
To beauty and to peace.

There in the early springtime
The violets are blue,

And adder-tongues in coats of gold
Are garmented anew.

There bayberry and aster
Are crowded on its floors,
When marching summer halts to praise
The Lord of Out-of-doors.

And there October passes
In gorgeous livery,—
In purple ash, and crimson oak,
And golden tulip tree.

And when the winds of winter
Their bugle blasts begin,
The snowy hosts of heaven arrive
And pitch their tents therein.

Bliss Carman

The Coming of Dawn

MIDNIGHT—the black, dead vast of night,
  Rain dripping slow on the sod,
Fear of the future, darkness-born,
  Doubt of myself and God.

A sudden flush on the face of night,
  A veil from my soul withdrawn,
A bird-note thrilling the silence through.
  And after that—the dawn.

Grace Atherton Dennen

Alms in Autumn

SPINDLE-WOOD, spindle-wood, will you lend me, pray,
A little flaming lantern to light me on my way?
The fairy folk have vanished from the meadow and the glen,
And I would fain go seeking till I find them once again;
Lend me now a lantern that I may bear a light
To show the hidden pathway in the darkness of the night.

Ash tree, ash tree, throw me, if you please,
Throw me down a slender bunch of russet-gold keys;
I fear the gates of fairyland may all be shut fast;
Give me of your magic keys that I may get past;
I'll tie them to my girdle, that as I go along
My heart may find a comfort in their tiny tinkling song.

Holly bush, holly bush, help me in my task,
A pocketful of berries is all the alms I ask;
A pocketful of berries to thread on glowing strands
(I would not go a-visiting with nothing in my hands);
So fine will be the rosy chains, so gay, so glossy bright,
They'll set the realms of fairyland a-dancing with delight.
Rose Fyleman

November in England

NO sun—no moon!
   No morn—no noon!
No dawn—no dusk—no proper time of day—
No sky—no earthly view—
No distance looking blue—
No road—no street—no "t'other side the way"—

No end to any "Row"—
No indications where the Crescents go—
No top to any steeple—
No recognitions of familiar people—
No courtesies for showing 'em—
No knowing 'em!
No travelling at all—no locomotion,
No inkling of the way—no notion—
"No go"—by land or ocean—
No mail—no post—
No news from any foreign coast—
No park—no ring—no afternoon gentility—
No company—no nobility—
No warmth, no cheerfulness, no healthful ease,
No comfortable feel in any member—
No shade, no shine, no butterflies, no bees,
No fruits, no flowers, no leaves, no birds,
November!

Thomas Hood

The Hound

SOME are sick for Spring and warm winds blowing
Over close-sheathed buds and a patch of old snow,
With the early arc-lamps delicately bowing
Across thin sunshine that hesitates to go.

But it's not for any April promises I sicken,
Though their stammering sweetness be a plucked string;
My mind is bent toward Autumn, I am shaken
More by her denials than by all the hopes of Spring.

The curt cold days, the blue and windy weather,
The smoke of burning brushwood keener than a frost,

An orchard full of odors night is wise to gather,
The fur-collared stubble where the flower is lost.

A clear green sunset and a pale moon showing,
A sense of dawning ends, like the light in the sky.
Autumn is a hound that shrills, my heart is for her gnawing,
The quarry goes to Autumn, let Spring die.
Babette Deutsch

Sky-Born Music

Evening in Tyringham Valley

WHAT domes and pinnacles of mist and fire
   Are builded in yon spacious realms of light
All silently, as did the walls aspire
   Templing the ark of God by day and night!
Noiseless and swift, from darkening ridge to ridge,
   Through purple air that deepens down the day,
Over the valley springs a shadowy bridge.
   The evening star's keen, solitary ray
Makes more intense the silence, and the glad,
   Unmelancholy, restful, twilight gloom—
So full of tenderness, that even the sad
   Remembrances that haunt the soul take bloom
Like that on yonder mountain.
                    Now the bars
   Of sunset all burn black; the day doth fail,
And the skies whiten with the eternal stars.
   O, let thy spirit stay with me, sweet vale!

Richard Watson Gilder

A Prairie Sunset

WHAT alchemist could in one hour so drain
   The rainbow of its colours, smelt the ore
From the September lodes of heaven, to pour
This Orient magic on a Western plain;
And build the miracle before our eyes
Of castellated heights and colonnades,
Carraran palaces, and cavalcades
Trooping throughout a city in the skies?
A northern cloud became a temple spire,
A southern reach showed argosies on fire;
And in the centre, with unhurried feet,
Came priests and paladins, soon to descend
To earth with swinging censers to attend
The God of harvests down amidst his wheat.

And scarcely less resplendent was the passing,
When with the night winds rising on the land
The hosts were led by a Valkyrian hand
To their abodes—accompanied by the massing
Of amber clouds touched with armorial red,
By thrones dissolving, and by spirals hurled
From golden plinths, announcing to the world
That Day, for all his blazonry, was dead.
And when, like a belated funeral rite,
The last pale torch was smothered by the night,
The mind's horizon like the sky was stripped
Of all allusion but a fable told
Of gods that died, of suns and worlds grown cold
In some extinct Promethean manuscript.

E. J. Pratt

Let Me Go Where'er I Will

LET me go where'er I will,
I hear a sky-born music still;
It sounds from all things old,
It sounds from all things young,
From all that's fair, from all that's foul,
Peals out a cheerful song.
It is not only in the rose,
It is not only in the bird,
Not only where the rainbow glows,
Nor in the song of woman heard,
But in the darkest, meanest things
There alway, alway something sings.
'T is not in the high stars alone,
Nor in the cups of budding flowers,
Nor in the red-breast's mellow tone,
Nor in the bow that smiles in showers,
But in the mud and scum of things
There alway, alway something sings.
  Ralph Waldo Emerson

Pippa's Song

THE year's at the spring,
And day's at the morn;
Morning's at seven;
The hill-side's dew-pearled.
The lark's on the wing;
The snail's on the thorn;
God's in his heaven—
All's right with the world!
  Robert Browning

The Whisper Of Earth

IN the misty hollow, shyly greening branches
  Soften to the South wind, bending to the rain.
From the moistened earthland flutter little whispers,
Breathing hidden beauty, innocent of stain.

Little plucking fingers tremble through the grasses,
Little silent voices sigh the dawn of spring,
Little burning earth-flames break the awful stillness,
Little crying wind-sounds come before the King.

Powers, dominations urge the budding of the crocus,
Cherubim are singing in the moist cool stone,
Seraphim are calling through the channels of the lily,
God has heard the earth-cry and journeys to His throne.
             Edward J. O'Brien

Sunrise

TODAY I saw the sun come up, like Neptune from the sea.
I saw him light a cliff with gold and wake a distant tree,
I saw him shake his shaggy head and laugh the night away
And toss unto a sleeping world another golden day.

The waves, which had been black and cold, came in with silver crests.
I saw the sunbeams gently wake the songbirds in their nests,
The slow-retreating night slipped back, and strewn on field and lawn,
On every blade of grass I saw the jewels of the dawn.

Never was monarch ushered in with such a cavalcade;
No hero bringing victory home has seen such wealth displayed.
In honor of the coming day, the humblest plant and tree
Stood on the curbstone of the world in radiant livery.

Pageants of splendor man may plan with robes of burnished gold,
On horses from Arabia may prance the knights of old;
Heralds on silver horns may blow, and kings come riding in,
But I have seen God's pageantry—I've watched a day begin!

Edgar A. Guest

Prayer Before Poems

GREAT Author of a world, of sky, of sea;
Whose lyrics are translated by the birds,
Come close and in the stillness I may learn
To worship Thee with words.

Thou, who dost guide all groping, gifted hands
'Till they can finger every helpless string
And find the souls of violins and harps,
Aid me to sing.

Artist, who did the great originals,
And carved the tender features of a saint,
Who chose the colors for a universe,
Teach me to paint.

Anne Blackwell Payne

How Miracles Abound

HOW miracles abound
   In each small plot of ground—
Aye, in the sky above it!
(Do you not love it,
The vast of sky a-thrill with lyric sound?)
Now comes, now goes,
The wonder of the rose;
Color or flower, and both a boon
Renewed with dawn or June.
Each day the hyacinthine twilight fills
The chalice of the hills.
Ever there's some fresh nectary
For the knight-errant bee.
And song—ah, the blithe bounty that sheds beauty
On the stern ways of duty!
Forsooth the doctrine's sound
That miracles abound!
E'en the green sod,
Yea, or the umbered clod,
Revealeth God!

Clinton Scollard

Little Things

THERE'S nothing very beautiful and nothing very gay
   About the rush of faces in the town by day,
But a light tan cow in a pale green mead,
That is very beautiful, beautiful indeed.
And the soft March wind and the low March mist

Are better than kisses in a dark street kissed. . . .
The fragrance of the forest when it wakes at dawn,
The fragrance of a trim green village lawn,
The hearing of the murmur of the rain at play—
These things are beautiful, beautiful as day!
And I shan't stand waiting for love or scorn
When the feast is laid for a day new-born. . . .
Oh, better let the little things I loved when little
Return when the heart finds the great things brittle;
And better is a temple made of bark and thong
Than a tall stone temple that may stand too long.
Orrick Johns

Clouds and Sky

ONE time when I was sick,
   And could but see
The sky above the top
Of a tall tree,

It first was coldly blue
Far past the tree.
Without a cloud, it seemed
Eternity.

But when clouds came, the sky,
(I know not how),
Was caught among the leaves—
And it was Now.

Lancaster Pollard

My Heart Leaps up When I Behold

MY heart leaps up when I behold
A rainbow in the sky:
So was it when my life began;
So is it now I am a man:
So be it when I shall grow old,
  Or let me die!
The Child is father of the Man—
And I could wish my days to be
Bound each to each by natural piety.
William Wordsworth

The Marshes

YE marshes, how candid and simple and nothing-withholding and free
Ye publish yourselves to the sky and offer yourselves to the sea!
Tolerant plains, that suffer the sea and the rains and the sun,
Ye spread and span like the catholic man who hath mightily won
God out of knowledge and good out of infinite pain
And sight out of blindness and purity out of a stain.

As the marsh-hen secretly builds on the watery sod,
Behold I will build me a nest on the greatness of God:
I will fly in the greatness of God as the marsh-hen flies
In the freedom that fills all the space 'twixt the marsh and the skies:

[1] Extract from "The Marshes of Glynn."

By so many roots as the marsh-grass sends in the sod
I will heartily lay me a-hold on the greatness of God:
Oh, like to the greatness of God is the greatness within
The range of the marshes, the liberal marshes of Glynn.
Sidney Lanier

Song

THE birds of the air, they sing it,
    Round the rim of the world they ring it;
The bees in the blossom-bell,
They tell, they tell.

No; birds in the air, none sing it,
For the rift of the dawn none ring it;
Noon bees in the blossom-bell,
None tell, none tell.

I say it over and over,—
There is none can speak for a lover;
But oh, ere the roses go,
Her heart will know!

John Vance Cheney

Out-of-Doors

WHAT came ye out for to seek, O Maker of Words?
    The color of grass in the sunshine, the music of birds;
And what shall ye do when ye find them, O Singer of Songs?
Weave a bright fabric of beauty, and give it to whom it belongs;

Weave a gay fabric of music, to lay at the feet of mankind,
All purple and gold for the sense, all golden and gray for
   the mind?

This came I out for to seek—the daffodil's gold,
The magic of buds all unfolding, the treasure untold
That lies in the heart of the forest, the moss and the leaves,
The jewel of flowers in the thicket, that no eye perceives;
And these will I weave into music, these will I fashion
   to words,
The wind in the grass and the rushes, the dawn-song of
   birds.

Ethel E. Mannin

The Whole Duty of Berkshire Brooks

To build the trout a crystal stair;
   To comb the hillside's thick green hair;
To water jewel-weed and rushes;
To teach first notes to baby thrushes;
To flavor raspberry and apple
And make a whirling pool to dapple
With scattered gold of late October;
To urge wise laughter on the sober
And lend a dream to those who laugh;
To chant the beetle's epitaph;
To mirror the blue dragonfly,
Frail air-plane of a slender sky;
Over the stones to lull and leap
Herding the bubbles like white sheep;
The claims of worry to deny,
And whisper sorrow into sleep!

Grace Hazard Conkling

A Word With a Skylark

IF this be all, for which I've listened long,
  Oh, spirit of the dew!
You did not sing to Shelley such a song
  As Shelley sang to you.

Yet, with this ruined Old World for a nest,
  Worm-eaten through and through,—
This waste of grave-dust stamped with crown and crest,—
  What better could you do?

Ah me! but when the world and I were young,
  There was an apple-tree,
There was a voice in the dawn that sung
  The buds awake—ah me!

Oh, Lark of Europe, downward fluttering near,
  Like some spent leaf at best,
You'd never sing again if you could hear
  My Bluebird of the West!

Sarah Piatt

The Perilous Light

THE Eternal Beauty smiled on me
  From the long lily's curvèd form,
She laughed in a wave of the sea,
She flashed on white wings through the storm.

In the bulb of a daffodil
She made a little joyful stir,
And the white cabin on the hill
Was my heart's home because of Her.

Her laughter fled the eyes of pride,
Barefoot She went o'er stony land,
And ragged children, hungry-eyed,
Clung to Her skirts and held Her hand.

When storm winds shook the cabin door
And red the Atlantic sunset blazed,
The fisher folk of Mullaghmore
Into Her eyes indifferent gazed.

By lonely waves She dwells apart,
And sea gulls circling on white wings,
Crowd round the windows of Her heart,
Most dear to Her of starving things.

The ploughman, down by Knocknarea,
Was free of Her twilight abode,
In shining sea-winds, salt with spray,
She haunted every gray cross road.

Some peasants with a creel of turf
Along the wind-swept boreen came,
Her feet went flashing through the surf,
Her wings were in the sunset's flame.

Beyond the rocks of Classiebawn,
The mackerel fishers sailing far,
Out in the vast Atlantic dawn
Found, tangled in their nets, a star.

In every spent and broken wave
The Eternal Beauty takes Her rest,
She is the Lover of the Brave,
The comrade of the perilous quest.

The Eternal Beauty wrung my heart,
Faithful is She, and true to shed
The austere glory of Art
On the scarceness of daily bread.

Men follow Her with toil and thought,
Over the heaven's starry pride,—
The Eternal Beauty comes unsought
To the child by the roadside.

Eva Gore-Booth

Folly

THE moon has made me weary
   With its silver and its song.
Such ardor in so old a thing
  Is wrong, all wrong.

It should be limping silently
  Across the leaden sky
Or grumbling at the cloud-hills
  The wind piles high.

It should be teaching little moons
  The proper way to shine,
Instead of singing sonnets
  To each adoring pine.

Vivian Yeiser Laramore

One Blackbird

THE stars must make an awful noise
  In whirling round the sky;

    Yet somehow I can't even hear
    Their loudest song or sigh.

    So it is wonderful to think
    One blackbird can outsing
    The voice of all the swarming stars
    On any day in spring.

Harold Monro

A Rune of Riches

I HAVE a golden ball,
  A big, bright, shining one,
Pure gold; and it is all
Mine.—It is the sun.

I have a silver ball,
A white and glistering stone
That other people call
The moon;—my very own!

The jewel things that prick
My cushion's soft blue cover
Are mine,—my stars, thick, thick,
Scattered the sky all over.

And everything that's mine
Is yours, and yours, and yours,—
The shimmer and the shine!—
Let's lock our wealth out-doors!

Florence Converse

The Picture

"THERE'S a pool in the ancient forest,"
  The painter-poet said,
"That is violet-blue and emerald
  From the face of the sky o'erhead."

So, far in the ancient forest,
  To the heart of the wood went I,
But found no pool of emerald,
  No violet-blue for sky.

"There's a pool in the ancient forest,"
  Said the painter-poet still.
"That is violet-blue and emerald,
  Near the breast of a rose-green hill."

And the heart of the ancient forest
  The painter-poet drew,
And painted a pool of emerald
  That thrilled me through and through.

Then back to the ancient forest
  I went with a strange, wild thrill,
And I found the pool of emerald,
  Near the breast of a rose-green hill.
    Frederick O. Sylvester

"Sic Vita"

HEART free, hand free,
  Blue above, brown under,
All the world to me

Is a place of wonder.
Sun shine, moon shine,
　　Stars, and winds a-blowing,
All into this heart of mine
　　Flowing, flowing, flowing!

Mind free, step free,
　　Days to follow after,
Joys of life sold to me
　　For the price of laughter.
Girl's love, man's love
　　Love of work and duty,
Just a will of God's to prove
　　Beauty, beauty, beauty!
　　　　　　　　William Stanley Braithwaite

A Blackbird Suddenly

HEAVEN is in my hand, and I
　　Touch a heart-beat of the sky,
Hearing a blackbird's cry.

Strange, beautiful, unquiet thing,
Lone flute of God, how can you sing
Winter to spring?

You have outdistanced every voice and word,
And given my spirit wings until it stirred
Like you—a bird!

　　　　　　　　Joseph Auslander

Credo

I BELIEVE
In the whispering of the peacock-plumaged sea,
In the moonshine and the little shining star,
I believe that in all color harmony
His angels are.

I believe
In the sunshine and the message of the flowers,
In the wind-song and the sea-song and the rain—
I believe that in summer's greening hours
God comes again.

Vera Wheatly

Gospel of the Fields

HAVE you ever thought, my friend,
As daily you toil and plod
In the noisy paths of man,
How still are the ways of God?

Have you ever paused in the din
Of traffic's insistent cry
To think of the calm in the cloud,
Of the peace in your glimpse of sky?

Go out in the growing fields
That quietly yield you meat,
And let them rebuke your noise
Whose patience is still and sweet.

They toil their æons—and we
  Who flutter back to their breast,
A handful of clamorous clay,
  Forget their silence is best!

Arthur Upson

The Welcome

GOD spreads a carpet soft and green
  O'er which we pass;
A thick-piled mat of jeweled sheen—
  And that is Grass.

Delightful music woos the ear;
  The grass is stirred
Down to the heart of every spear—
  Ah, that's a Bird.

Clouds roll before a blue immense
  That stretches high
And lends the soul exalted sense—
  That scroll's a Sky.

Green rollers flaunt their sparkling crests;
  Their jubilee
Extols brave Captains and their quests—
  And that is Sea.

New-leaping grass, the feathery flute,
  The sapphire ring,
The sea's full-voiced, profound salute,—
  Ah, this is Spring!

Arthur Powell

Angels of the Spring

WE see them not—we cannot hear
    The music of their wing—
Yet know we that they sojourn near,
    The angels of the spring!

They glide along this lovely ground
    When the first violet grows;
Their graceful hands have just unbound
    The zone of yonder rose.

I gather it for thy dear breast,
    From stain and shadow free:
That which an Angel's love hath blest
    Is meet, my love, for thee!

Robert Stephen Hawkes

God's World

O WORLD, I cannot hold thee close enough!
    Thy winds, thy wide gray skies!
    Thy mists that roll and rise!
Thy woods, this autumn day, that ache and sag
And all but cry with color! That gaunt crag
To crush! To lift the lean of that black bluff!
World, World, I cannot get thee close enough!

Long have I known a glory in it all,
    But never knew I this;
    Here such a passion is
As stretcheth me apart. Lord, I do fear

Thou'st made the world too beautiful this year.
My soul is all but out of me,—let fall
No burning leaf; prithee, let no bird call.
>> *Edna St. Vincent Millay*

Rain

I NEVER knew how words were vain
   Until I strove to say
The thoughts that fell like the gray rain
   Upon my heart today.

The April rain falls on the earth,
   That waits a while for words,
And then becomes articulate
   In buds and bees and birds.

The thoughts that rain upon my heart
   Bring nothing fair to birth;
O God, I kneel before the art,
   Of this great lyrist, earth.
>> *Kenneth Slade Alling*

The Lark

(*Salisbury, England*)

A CLOSE gray sky,
   And poplars gray and high,
The country-side along;
The steeple bold

Across the acres old—
And then a song!

Oh, far, far, far,
As any spire or star,
Beyond the cloistered wall!
Oh, high, high, high,
A heart-throb in the sky—
Then not at all!

Lizette Woodworth Reese

Farewell

TELL them, O Sky-born, when I die
  With high romance to wife,
That I went out as I had lived,
  Drunk with the joy of life.

Yea, say that I went down to death
  Serene and unafraid,
Still loving Song, but loving more
  Life, of which Song is made!

Harry Kemp

The Comfort of the Stars

WHEN I am overmatched by petty cares
  And things of earth loom large, and look to be
Of moment, how it soothes and comforts me
To step into the night and feel the airs

Of heaven fan my cheek; and, best of all,
  Gaze up into those all-uncharted seas
  Where swim the stately planets: such as these
Make mortal fret seem light and temporal.

I muse on what of Life may stir among
  Those spaces knowing naught of metes nor bars;
  Undreamed-of dramas played in outmost stars,
And lyrics by archangels grandly sung.

I grow familiar with the solar runes
  And comprehend of worlds the mystic birth;
  Ringed Saturn, Mars, whose fashion apes the earth,
And Jupiter, the giant, with his moons.

Then, dizzy with the unspeakable sights above,
  Rebuked by Vast on Vast, my puny heart
  Is greatened for its transitory part,
My trouble merged in wonder and in love.

Richard Burton

The Last Hour

O JOYS of love and joys of fame,
  It is not you I shall regret:
  I sadden lest I should forget
The beauty woven in earth's name.

The shout and battle of the gale,
  The stillness of the sun-rising,
  The sound of some deep hidden spring,
The glad sob of the filling sail,

The first green ripple of the wheat,
  The rain-song of the lifted leaves,
  The waking birds beneath the eaves,
The voices of the summer heat.

Ethel Clifford

Wasted Hours

THERE was a day I wasted long ago,
  Lying upon a hillside in the sun—
An April day of wind and drifting clouds,
An idle day and all my work undone.

The little peach trees with their coral skirts
Were dancing up the hillside in the breeze;
The gray walled meadows gleamed like bits of jade
Against the crimson bloom of maple trees.

And I could smell the warmth of trodden grass,
The coolness of a freshly harrowed field;
And I could hear a bluebird's wistful song
Of love and beauty only half revealed.

I have forgotten many April days
But one there is that comes to haunt me still—
A day of feathered trees and windy skies
And wasted hours on a sunlit hill.

Medora Addison

God is at the Anvil

GOD is at the anvil, beating out the sun;
  Where the molten metal spills,

At His forge among the hills
He has hammered out the glory of a day that's done.

God is at the anvil, welding golden bars;
In the scarlet-streaming flame
He is fashioning a frame
For the shimmering silver beauty of the evening stars.
Lew Sarett

At the End of the Trail

Time and Spirit

SPIRIT going with me here,
If thou tellest time aright,
It's by some ancestral clock
Older than the golden sun,
And his measure trod with night.

Rarely by my calendar
Bite or sup for thee is spread,
Yet thou comst not grace forgone
As the jostling starvelings do,
But most mannerly art fed.

Half my store consumes to keep
This poor lamp which warmeth me.
Thou takst no thought to live
In a delicate excess
Spendst more brightness than I see.

How should thou and I keep step?
Three score ten was set my race
Of just distancing the worm;
But a lifetime to a sphere
Lends a more exalted pace.

Léonie Adams

The Full Heart

ALONE on the shore in the pause of the nightime
   I stand and I hear the long wind blow light;
I view the constellations quietly, quietly burning
I hear the wave fall in the hush of the night.

Long after I am dead, ended this bitter journey,
Many another whose heart holds no light
Shall your solemn sweetness hush, awe, and comfort,
O my companions, Wind, Waters, Stars, and Night.
Robert Nichols

That Time of Year

THAT time of year thou mayst in me behold
   When yellow leaves, or none, or few, do hang
Upon those boughs which shake against the cold,
Bare ruined choirs, where late the sweet birds sang.
In me thou see'st the twilight of such day
As after sunset fadeth in the west,
Which by and by black night doth take away,
Death's second self, that seals up all in rest.
In me thou see'st the glowing of such fire
That on the ashes of his youth doth lie,
As the death-bed whereon it must expire,
Consumed with that which it was nourished by.
This thou perceiv'st, which makes thy love more strong,
To love that well which thou must leave ere long.
William Shakespeare

Hesperides

BEYOND the blue rim of the world,
  Washed round with languid-lapsing seas,
Where the Wind's wings were ever furled
  The Ancients dreamed Hesperides.

Ship after ship each age sent forth
  To find the Islands of the Blest;
The loosed winds drove them south and north,
  But west they weathered, ever west.

Sky after sky they dropped behind,
  Those mighty-handed, bearded men,
Till, seeking what they could not find,
  They rounded upward, home again.

A desultory waif of time
  Flying adventure from my mast,
'Twas thus I voyaged every clime
  To come back to myself at last!

Harry Kemp

Changeless

THEY cannot change the hills; though they may hew
  The fir-sweet slopes and cut their roadways through,
Yet will they stand, each long-loved mountain face
And smile at me from its appointed place;
And past their friendly crests the sun shall rise
To paint new pictures on the morning skies—
  They cannot change the hills.

They cannot still the winds; the winds that shake
The hemlock fragrance free and sweep the lake,
The waves at dusk shall whisper to the shore
Their pebbled secrets as they did before;
The wild white clouds as in the days of old
Shall sink to rest in sunset seas of gold—
    They cannot still the winds.

They cannot dim the stars; the crowding camps
That dot the dusk with closely-clustered lamps,
The jazz, the laughter, and the shrill tin blare
Of phonographs, the motor headlight's flare—
These shall be stilled at last—the clamor cease
And leave a fir-sweet world of wave-lapped peace—
    They cannot dim the stars!

Martha Haskell Clark

Homesick

O MY garden! lying whitely in the moonlight and the dew,
Far across the leagues of distance flies my heart to-night to you,
And I see your stately lilies in the tender radiance gleam
With a dim, mysterious splendor, like the angels of a dream!

I can see the stealthy shadows creep along the ivied wall,
And the bosky depths of verdure where the drooping vine-leaves fall,
And the tall trees standing darkly with their crowns against the sky,
While overhead the harvest moon goes slowly sailing by.

I can see the trellised arbor, and the roses' crimson glow,
And the lances of the larkspurs all glittering, row on row,
And the wilderness of hollyhocks, where brown bees seek
  their spoil,
And butterflies dance all day long, in glad and gay turmoil.

Oh, the broad paths running straightly, north and south and
  east and west!
Oh, the wild grape climbing sturdily to reach the oriole's
  nest!
Oh, the bank where wild flowers blossom, ferns nod and
  mosses creep
In a tangled maze of beauty over all the wooded steep!

Just beyond the moonlit garden I can see the orchard trees,
With their dark boughs overladen, stirring softly in the
  breeze,
And the shadows on the greensward, and within the pasture
  bars
The white sheep huddling quietly beneath the pallid stars.

With a vague, half-startled wonder if some night in Paradise,
From the battlements of heaven I shall turn my longing eyes
All the dim, resplendent spaces and the mazy stardrifts
  through
To my garden lying whitely in the moonlight and the dew!
Julia C. R. Dorr

If all the Skies

IF all the skies were sunshine,
  Our faces would be fain
To feel once more upon them
  The cooling plash of rain.

If all the world were music,
  Our hearts would often long
For one sweet strain of silence,
  To break the endless song.

If life were always merry,
  Our souls would seek relief,
And rest from weary laughter
  In the quiet arms of grief.

Henry van Dyke

"Gratias Age"

SINCE of earth, air and water,
  The gods have made me part—
Let every human sin be mine
Except the thankless heart!
Privileged and greatly, I partake
Of sleep and death and birth;
And kneeling, drink the sacrament—
The good red wine of earth.

I shall not ask the High Gods
For aught that they can give;
They gave the greatest gift of all
When first they bade me live.
Great gift of dawn and starlight,
Of sea and grass and river;
With leave to toil and laugh and weep
And praise the Sun forever!

Be death the end or not the end,
Too richly blest am I

To seek the hill behind the hill,
The sky behind the sky.
Let the red earth that bore me
Give me her call again,
And I'll lie still beneath her flowers
And sleep and not complain.

Let those the gods have blinded
Hold their long feud with Fate—
And clutch at toys that never yet
Could make one mean man great.
Let those that Earth has bastarded
Fret and contrive and plan—
But I will enter like an heir
The old estate of man!

Geoffrey Howard

Song of Ballyshannon

TAKE me home to Ballyshannon, for there's music in the word;
The name o' Ballyshannon is the sweetest ever heard!
The little hills are lying fair and green behind the town,
And the skies of Ballyshannon, why, they're never known to frown.
Take me back and let me hearken to the plaintive Irish wind;
Take me back to Ballyshannon, where the neighbors' hearts are kind.

I will wander in the moonlight out upon the ragged moor,
With the flaming gorse and heather,—I'll not find it mean or poor.

In the glen with lads a-dancing, I will pass the night away;
For the nights in Ballyshannon, they are sweeter than the day.
Take me back to Ballyshannon, there's a voice that calls to me;
For my heart's in Ballyshannon on the other side the sea.

I came to Ballyshannon on a wet and mournful night,
And all the way was darkness, with never a ray of light;
The mist was waving round me and the winds were blowing free
When I came to Ballyshannon, sure my heart was whole in me.

I went from Ballyshannon when the sun was rolling high,
And every rowan bud was glad and looked me in the eye;
The clouds were white above me and the winds played in the tree,
Yet I went from Ballyshannon bearing little heart in me.

Sure my heart was crushed and broken; there were kisses on my mouth;
There were cruel words upon me like a summer's parching drouth.
Woman's wiles are full of mystery, they're inconstant as the sea;
Just for sport in Ballyshannon, someone stole the heart of me.

The bells of Ballyshannon, I hear them on the wind,
And every care and sorrow my heart leaves far behind;
I can live and thrive a season upon an alien shore,
But I'm wanting Ballyshannon forever all the more;
And when light o' life has left me and I'm like an empty byre,

Lay my bones in Ballyshannon, take me back to heart's desire,
Where I'll hear the bells a-ringing, folded arms beneath the sod,
For the bells of Ballyshannon, they will ring me home to God.

Jeanne Robert Foster

A Song of the Road

I LIFT my cap to Beauty,
   I lift my cap to Love;
I bow before my Duty,
   And know that God's above!
My heart through shining arches
   Of leaf and blossom goes;
My soul, triumphant, marches
   Through life to life's repose.
And I, through all this glory,
   Nor know, nor fear my fate,—
The great things are so simple,
   The simple are so great!

Fred G. Bowles

After Sunset

I HAVE an understanding with the hills
   At evening when the slanted radiance fills
Their hollows, and the great winds let them be,
And they are quiet and look down at me.
Oh, then I see the patience in their eyes

Out of the centuries that made them wise.
They lend me hoarded memory and I learn
Their thoughts of granite and their whims of fern,
And why a dream of forests must endure
Though every tree be slain: and how the pure,
Invisible beauty has a word so brief
A flower can say it or a shaken leaf,
But few may ever snare it in a song,
Though for the quest a life is not too long.
When the blue hills grow tender, when they pull
The twilight close with gesture beautiful,
And shadows are their garments, and the air
Deepens, and the wild veery is at prayer,—
Their arms are strong around me; and I know
That somehow I shall follow when you go
To the still land beyond the evening star,
Where everlasting hills and valleys are:
And silence may not hurt us any more,
And terror shall be past, and grief, and war.
Grace Hazard Conkling

The Wanderer

THE ships are lying in the bay,
   The gulls are swinging round their spars;
My soul as eagerly as they
   Desires the margin of the stars.

So much do I love wandering,
   So much I love the sea and sky,
That it will be a piteous thing
   In one small grave to lie.

Zoe Akins

The Trumpet of The Dawn

ABOVE the crestward-climbing pines,
  Above the dewy slopes of lawn,
Above the copse's coil of vines,
  I have gone up to meet the dawn.

I have grown weary of the night
  That from day's gold mine eye debars,—
Of seeing up the purple height
  Troop the processional of stars.

I yearn to mark the shattering beam
  Backward the gates of darkness throw;
I long to hear across my dream
  The wakening trump of morning blow.

Hark! 'tis the first bird-note!—and mark,
  Flushing the east, a crimson ray!—
Soul, from the girdling wastes of dark
  Go thou, too, up to meet the day!
Clinton Scollard

Shared

I SAID it in the meadow-path,
  I say it on the mountain-stairs,—
The best things any mortal hath
  Are those which every mortal shares.

The air we breathe, the sky, the breeze,
  The light without us and within,—

Life, with its unlocked treasures,—
   God's riches,—are for all to win.

The grass is softer to my tread
   For rest it yields unnumbered feet;
Sweeter to me the wild-rose red,
   Because she makes the whole world sweet.

. . . .

And up the radiant, peopled way,
   That opens into worlds unknown,
It will be life's delight to say,
   "Heaven is not Heaven for me alone."
Lucy Larcom

Up-hill

DOES the road wind-up all the way?
   Yes, to the very end.
Will the day's journey take the whole long day?
   From morn to night, my friend.

But is there for the night a resting-place?
   A roof for when the slow dark hours begin?
May not the darkness hide it from my face?
   You cannot miss that inn.

Shall I meet other wayfarers at night?
   Those who have gone before.
Then must I knock, or call when just in sight?
   They will not keep you standing at that door.

Shall I find comfort, travel-sore and weak?
   Of labor you shall find the sum.

Will there be beds for me and all who seek?
Yea, beds for all who come.
Christina Rossetti

The Epitaph

WRITE on my grave when I am dead,
    Whatever road I trod
That I admired and honorèd
The wondrous works of God.

That all the days and years I had,
The greatest and the least,
Each day with grateful heart and glad
I sat me to a feast.

That not alone for body's meat
Which takes the lowest place
I gave Him grace when I did eat
And with a shining face.

But for the spirit filled and fed
That else must waste and die,
With sun and stars replenishèd
And dew and evening sky.

The beauty of the hills and seas
Brimmed that immortal cup;
And when I went by fields and trees
My heart was lifted up.

Lap me in the green grass and write
Upon the daisied sod
That still I praised with all my might
The wondrous works of God.
Katharine Tynan

White Armour

DEMAND no bay or laurel now
  To wrap about thy lifted brow,

But as the fated hour nears,
Accept a chaplet of my tears.

And this, to clasp thy traveller's hood,
The ruby of my frozen blood.

As mantle for thy wayward breast
My weakness will, I think, be best.

My strength, thy staff that does not bend,
Will serve to slay me at the end.

My night and morning prayers to God,
Twin sandals wherewith thou art shod.

My love—which bends before His Wrath,
Sweet grass to ease thy stony path.
  Jean Starr Untermeyer

Shepherds Who Pastures Seek

SHEPHERDS who pastures seek
  At dawn may see
From Falterona's peak
  Above Camaldoli
Shine, over forests ranged and wildernesses bleak,
  Both shores of Italy.
Open your gates, O clouds of the morning,
  And, men, lift up your eyes!

And scarce can eye see light
   When the ear's aware
That instruments exquisite
   Are raining from the air—
While sun and pale moon mingle their delight—
   Adorations everywhere.
Open your gates, O sons of the morning,
   And, men, lift up your eyes!

Halo of golden dust—
   Eddy of rays
Thrilling up, up, as they must
   Die of the life they praise—
The larks, the larks! that to the Earth entrust
   Only their sleeping-place.
Open your gates, O mists of the morning,
   And, men, lift up your eyes!

Opens Night's blue Pantheon
   Its dark roof-ring
For that escaping paean
   Of tremblers on the wing
At the unknown threshold of the empyrean
   In myriads soft to sing,
Open your gates, O sons of the morning,
   And, men, lift up your eyes!

Hark! it grows less and less—
   But nothing mars
That rapture beyond guess—
   Beyond our senses' bars—
They drink the virgin Light, the measureless,
   And in it fade, like stars.
Open your gates, O deeps of the Morning,
   And, Men, lift up your eyes!

Between two lamps suspended,
   Of Life and Death,
Sun-marshalled and moon-tended
   Man's swift soul journeyeth
To be borne out of the life, it hath transcended
   Still, still on a breath!
Open your gates, O sons of the Morning,
   O men, lift up your eyes!

Herbert Trench

Good-Bye

GOOD-BYE, proud world! I'm going home:
   Thou art not my friend, and I'm not thine.
Long through thy weary crowds I roam;
A river-ark on the ocean brine,
Long I've been tossed like the driven foam;
But now, proud world! I'm going home.

Good-bye to Flattery's fawning face;
To Grandeur with his wise grimace;
To upstart Wealth's averted eye;
To supple Office, low and high;
To crowded halls, to court and street;
To frozen hearts and hasting feet;
To those who go, and those who come;
Good-bye, proud world! I'm going home.

I am going to my own hearth-stone,
Bosomed in yon green hills along,—
A secret nook in a pleasant land,
Whose groves the frolic fairies planned;
Where arches green, the livelong day,
Echo the blackbird's roundelay,
And vulgar feet have never trod
A spot that is sacred to thought and God.

O, when I am safe in my sylvan home,
I tread on the pride of Greece and Rome;
And when I am stretched beneath the pines,
Where the evening star so holy shines,
I laugh at the lore and the pride of man,
At the sophist schools, and the learned clan;
For what are they all, in their high conceit,
When man in the bush with God may meet?
                    Ralph Waldo Emerson

The Day Is Done

THE day is done, and the darkness
  Falls from the wings of Night,
As a feather is wafted downward
  From an eagle in his flight.

I see the lights of the village
  Gleam through the rain and the mist,
And a feeling of sadness comes o'er me
  That my soul cannot resist:

A feeling of sadness and longing,
  That is not akin to pain,
And resembles sorrow only
  As the mist resembles the rain.

Come, read to me some poem,
  Some simple and heartfelt lay,
That shall soothe this restless feeling,
  And banish the thoughts of day.

Not from the grand old masters,
  Not from the bards sublime,
Whose distant footsteps echo
  Through the corridors of Time.

For, like strains of martial music,
  Their mighty thoughts suggest
Life's endless toil and endeavor;
  And tonight I long for rest.

Read from some humbler poet,
  Whose songs gushed from his heart,
As showers from the clouds of summer,
  Or tears from the eyelids start;

Who, through long days of labor,
  And nights devoid of ease,
Still heard in his soul the music
  Of wonderful melodies.

Such songs have power to quiet
  The restless pulse of care,
And come like the benediction
  That follows after prayer.

Then read from the treasured volume
  That poem of thy choice,
And lend to the rhyme of the poet
  The beauty of thy voice.

And the night shall be filled with music,
  And the cares, that infest the day,
Shall fold their tents, like the Arabs,
  And as silently steal away.
                        Henry Wadsworth Longfellow

Memory

WHEN I was young my heart and head were light,
  And I was gay and feckless as a colt
Out in the fields, with morning in the may,
Wind on the grass, wings in the orchard bloom.
  O thrilling sweet, my joy, when life was free,

    And all the paths led on from hawthorn-time
    Across the carolling meadows into June.

But now my heart is heavy-laden. I sit
Burning my dreams away beside the fire;
And I am rich in all that I have lost.
    O starshine on the fields of long-ago,
    Bring me the darkness and the nightingale;
    Dim wealds of vanished summer, peace of home,
    And silence: and the faces of my friends.

Siegfried Sassoon

Hark! Hark!

NO sight of it, only the song,
    Hours long;
Hidden in the sun, yet near—
See, see the tiny trilling dot appear,
To disappear!

As if a pranking star had lowered it
By a thread
Over the listener's head,
(Scarce swinging),
And then
Had pulled it up again,
Up, up, to the impenetrable blue,
And through—
Still singing!

Leonora Speyer

The Noise of Leaves

ALIVE in space against his will,
    A man may find along his way
Some loveliness to live for still:

He falls upon the earth in May
And hides his face from the cold moon
Whose beauty mocks him when he grieves,
And hears the birds subside, and soon
Only the noise of blowing leaves,

And wonders why his heart grows light
To hear the soft contagion spread
From tree to tree across the night.
He knows that even the jointless dead
Are not so lonely where they sprawl,
Yet knows that he is not alone—

He clings to something after all,
Stretched on a flying flowering stone.

George Dillon

Far in a Western Brookland

FAR in a western brookland
   That bred me long ago
The poplars stand and tremble
   By pools I used to know.

There, in the windless night-time,
   The wanderer, marvelling why,
Halts on the bridge to hearken
   How soft the poplars sigh.

He hears: no more remembered
   In fields where I was known,
Here I lie down in London
   And turn to rest alone.

There, by the starlit fences,
   The wanderer halts and hears
My soul that lingers sighing
   About the glimmering weirs.
A. E. Housman

I Am Weary of Being Bitter

I AM weary of being bitter and weary of being wise,
   And the armour and the mask of these fall from me, after long.
I would go where the islands sleep, or where the sea-dawns rise,
   And lose my bitter wisdom in the wisdom of a song.

There are magics in melodies, unknown of the sages;
   The powers of purest wonder on secret wings go by.
Doubtless out of the silence of dumb preceding ages
   Song woke the chaos-world—and light swept the sky.

All that we know is idle; idle is all we cherish;
   Idle the will that takes loads that proclaim it strong.
For the knowledge, the strength, the burden—all shall perish:
   One thing only endures, one thing only—song.
Arthur D. Ficke

Death — Divination

DEATH is like moonlight in a lofty wood,
   That pours pale magic through the shadowy leaves;
'T is like the web that some old perfume weaves
In a dim, lonely room where memories brood,
Like snow-chilled wine it steals into the blood,
   Spurring the pulse its coolness half reprieves;

Tenderly quickening impulses it gives,
As April winds unsheathe an opening bud.

Death is like all sweet, sense-enfolding things,
  That lift us in a dream-delicious trance
  Beyond the flickering good and ill of chance;
But most is Death like Music's buoyant wings,
  That bear the soul, a willing Ganymede,
  Where joys on joys forevermore succeed.

Charles Wharton Stork

Thanks

THANK you very much indeed,
  River, for your waving reed;
Hollyhocks, for budding knobs;
Foxgloves, for your velvet fobs;
Pansies, for your silky cheeks
Chaffinches, for singing beaks;
Spring, for wood anemones
Near the mossy toe of trees;
Summer, for the fruited pear
Yellowing crab, and cherry fare;
Autumn, for the bearded load,
Hazelnuts along the road;
Winter, for the fairy-tale,
Splitting log and bouncing hail.

But, blest Father, high above,
All these joys are from Thy love;
And Your children everywhere,
Born in palace, lane, or square,
Cry with voices all agreed,
"Thank You very much indeed."

Norman Gale

Index by Authors

Abbey, Henry, 69
Adams, Léonie, 60, 255
Addison, Medora, 253
Akins, Zoe, 264
Alling, Kenneth Slade, 250
Allingham, William, 44
Auslander, Joseph, 124, 246

Baker, Karl Wilson, 71
Banning, Kendall, 162
Bates, Katharine Lee, 36, 172
Birchall, Sara Hamilton, 55, 57, 139, 144, 146, 156, 165, 175, 223
Blanden, Charles G., 42
Bowles, Fred G., 263
Braithwaite, William Stanley, 245
Brotherton, Alice Williams, 49
Brown, Mabel, 38
Brown, Thomas E., 41
Browning, Robert, 94, 212, 233
Burnet, Dana, 157
Burton, Richard, 95, 211, 216, 251
Byron, Lord, 100

Carman, Bliss, 17, 49, 53, 65, 75, 119, 136, 168, 171, 173, 176, 186, 200, 220, 226
Chalmers, Stephens, 140
Cheney, John Vance, 41, 239
Clark, Martha Haskell, 91, 104, 161, 257
Clifford, Ethel, 252
Clough, Arthur Hugh, 151
Cole, Samuel Valentine, 67
Cone, Helen Gray, 51, 56
Conkling, Grace Hazard, 240, 263

Converse, Florence, 244
Craik, Dina Mulock, 42
Crane, Jr. L. Burton, 28
Crapsey, Adelaide, 153
Cunningham, Allan, 87

Davis, Fannie Stearns, 120, 158
Davies, Mary Carolyn, 163
Davies, William H., 1, 76, 112
Dean, Harry W., 171
Dennen, Grace Atherton, 227
Deutsch, Babette, 229
Dickinson, Emily, 54, 118, 130, 210, 218, 225
Dillon, George, 273
Dorr, Julia C. R., 258
Driscoll, Louise, 5, 40, 189

Egbert, Ella Elizabeth, 224
Elliston, George, 210
Emerson, Ralph Waldo, 52, 191, 233, 270

Fenton, Cora D., 31
Ficke, Arthur Davison, 275
Foster, Jeanne Robert, 261
Fox-Smith, C., 133, 147
Frost, Frances, 59
Fyleman, Rose, 228

Gale, Norman, 35, 193, 276
Galsworthy, John, 110
Garland, Hamlin, 4, 109
Garrison, Theodosia, 15, 18, 114, 125, 175, 195, 219
Gilder, Richard Watson, 181, 231
Gilman, Charlotte Perkins, 61
Gore-Booth, Eva, 78, 241
Gould, Gerald, 155

Grover, Edwin Osgood, 135, 185
Guest, Edgar A., 10, 16, 34, 150, 155, 169, 234
Guiney, Louise Imogen, 53
Guiterman, Arthur, 121, 129

Hagedorn, Hermann, 143
Hardy, Thomas, 184
Hare, Amory, 23
Hawkes, Robert Stephen, 249
Higginson, Ella, 203
Hood, Thomas, 228
Hopper, Nora, 81
Housman, A. E., 274
Hovey, Richard, 12, 31, 79, 92, 122, 196
Howard, Geoffrey, 260
Hoyt, Helen, 132
Hubbell, Rose Strong, 37

Jennings, Leslie Nelson, 8
Johns, Orrick, 236

Kauffman, Ruth Wright, 165
Kemp, Harry, 77, 115, 134, 199, 213, 251, 257
Kenyon, Theda, 50
Ketchum, Arthur, 111, 131
King, Georgiana Goddard, 19
Kipling, Rudyard, 166
Knowles, Frederic Lawrence, 102

Lanier, Sidney, 66, 238
Laramore, Vivian Yeiser, 243
Larcom, Lucy, 44, 71, 160, 265
Laurence, Ray, 48
Le Gallienne, Richard, 111
Longfellow, Henry Wadsworth, 271
Loveman, Robert, 209
Lowell, James Russell, 45

Mackay, Isabel Ecclestine, 19
MacLeish, Archibald, 108
Macleod, Fiona, 88
McGiffert, Gertrude Huntington, 27
McGroarty, John Steven, 32, 99
McLeod, Irene Rutherford, 126
McQuilland, Louis J., 25
Mannin, Ethel E., 80, 150, 178, 239
Markham, Edwin, 57
Masefield, John, 3, 75
Mason, Caroline Atherton, 112
Meynell, Alice, 107
Millay, Edna St. Vincent, 125, 145, 249
Millay, Kathleen, 2, 60
Miller, Marjorie Alice, 105
Monro, Harold, 243
Montgomery, James Stuart, 22, 82, 104
Moreland, John Richard, 193
Morley, Christopher, 68

Nash, Ogden, 153
Nichols, Robert, 256
Norton, Eleanour, 29

O'Brien, Edward J., 234
O'Reilly, John Boyle, 7

Payne, Anne Blackwell, 235
Peace, Dorothy, 103
Percy, William Alexander, 218
Piatt, Sarah, 241
Pickthall, Marjorie, 179
Pollard, Lancaster, 144, 186, 192, 237
Powell, Arthur, 248
Pratt, E. J., 232
Procter, Bryan Waller, 89

Randolph, Thomas, 30
Reese, Lizette Woodworth, 194, 250
Rice, Cale Young, 86, 115, 182, 188, 196
Rittenhouse, Jessie B., 72
Roberts, Charles G. D., 39, 89
Robinson, Corinne Roosevelt, 9
Rossetti, Christina, 110, 266
Runcie, John, 85
Russell, Maud, 29

Sandburg, Carl, 74
Sarett, Lew, 253
Sassoon, Siegfried, 107, 272
Scollard, Clinton, 43, 73, 149, 183, 190, 236, 265
Service, Robert W., 13
Shakespeare, William, 256
Shepard, Odell, 3
Slender, Pauline, 164
Smith, Ada, 20
Smith, May Riley, 142, 213
Speyer, Leonora, 62, 215, 273
Stork, Charles Wharton, 275
Stuart, Keith, 82
Swinburne, Algernon Charles, 97
Sylvester, Frederick O., 245

Tabb, John B., 55
Tennyson, Alfred, 205, 212

Thorley, Wilfrid C., 47
Tietjens, Eunice, 127
Timrod, Henry, 109, 206
Tinckom-Fernandez, W. G., 24, 177
Towne, Charles Hanson, 6, 195, 219
Trench, Herbert, 62, 268
Tynan, Katherine, 96, 183, 267

Unknown, 63, 100
Untermeyer, Jean Starr, 118, 268
Untermeyer, Louis, 36
Upson, Arthur, 247

van Dyke, Henry, 70, 259
Vinal, Harold, 84

Waterman, Nixon, 148
Watson, William, 208
Welby, Amelia C., 103
Welles, Winifred, 117
Wetherald, Ethelwyn, 64
Wheatly, Vera, 247
Whitman, Walt, 9, 47, 84
Widdemer, Margaret, 79, 113
Williams, Oscar, 85
Wolfe, Humbert, 48, 54
Wordsworth, William, 21, 94, 238

Index by Titles

A.B.C.'s in Green .... *Leonora Speyer*, 62
Afoot .... *Charles G. D. Roberts*, 39
Afoot .... *C. Fox-Smith*, 133
Afoot and Light-Hearted .... *Walt Whitman*, 9
Afternoon on a Hill .... *Edna St. Vincent Millay*, 125
After Sunset .... *Grace Hazard Conkling*, 240
Again Among the Hills .... *Richard Hovey*, 122
"A la Belle Ètoile" .... *Sara Hamilton Birchall*, 144
Alms in Autumn .... *Rose Fyleman*, 228
An Autumn Garden .... *Bliss Carman*, 220
Angels of the Spring .... *Robert Stephen Hawkes*, 249
Answer, The .... *Sara Hamilton Birchall*, 57
April .... *Emily Dickinson*, 210
April .... *John Vance Cheney*, 41
April .... *Theodosia Garrison*, 195
April, April .... *William Watson*, 208
April's Coming .... *Lancaster Pollard*, 192
April Morning .... *George Elliston*, 210
April Music .... *Clinton Scollard*, 183
April Rain .... *Robert Loveman*, 209
April Weather .... *Lizette Woodworth Reese*, 194
April Weather .... *Bliss Carman*, 186
As the Tide Comes In .... *Cale Young Rice*, 86
Autumn .... *Emily Dickinson*, 218

Bag-Piles at Sea .... *Clinton Scollard*, 73
Beloved Vagabond, The .... *W. G. Tinckom-Fernandez*, 177
Best Road of All, The .... *Charles Hanson Towne*, 6
Black Ashes .... *Martha Haskell Clark*, 161
Blackbird, The .... *Humbert Wolfe*, 54
Blackbird Suddenly, A .... *Joseph Auslander*, 246
Blind .... *Harry Kemp*, 199
Bring Me the Sunset in a Cup .... *Emily Dickinson*, 130
Buttercups .... *Wilfrid C. Thorley*, 47

Call, The .... *Cora D. Fenton*, 31
Call, The .... *Edgar A. Guest*, 150
Call of the Wild, The .... *Robert W. Service*, 13
Camping Song .... *Bliss Carman*, 17

280

Carouse .... *Charles Hanson Towne*, 219
Changeless .... *Martha Haskell Clark*, 257
City Voice, A .... *Theodosia Garrison*, 15
City-Weary .... *Edgar A. Guest*, 10
Climb, The .... *Winifred Welles*, 117
Clover .... *John B. Tabb*, 55
Clouds and Sky .... *Lancaster Pollard*, 237
Come, Spur Away .... *Thomas Randolph*, 30
Comfort of the Stars, The .... *Richard Burton*, 251
Coming of Dawn, The .... *Grace Atherton Dennen*, 227
Comrades of the Trail .... *Mary Carolyn Davies*, 163
Conversation, A .... *Sara Hamilton Birchall*, 55
Cook County .... *Archibald MacLeish*, 108
Country Faith, The .... *Norman Gale*, 35
Coquette .... *Keith Stuart*, 82
Credo .... *Vera Wheatley*, 247
Cry of the Dreamers, The .... *John Boyle O'Reilley*, 7
Cry of the Hillborn, The .... *Bliss Carman*, 119

Daisies .... *Bliss Carman*, 53
Dandelions, The .... *Helen Gray Cone*, 51
Dandelion, To the .... *James Russell Lowell*, 45
Day Is Done, The .... *Henry Wadsworth Longfellow*, 271
Days Like These .... *Ella Elizabeth Egbert*, 224
Deep Down .... *James Stuart Montgomery*, 104
Death—Divination .... *Charles Wharton Stork*, 275
Deep-Water Man, The .... *James Stuart Montgomery*, 82
Denial .... *Lancaster Pollard*, 144
Deserted Pasture, The .... *Bliss Carman*, 226
Down East and Up Along .... *Edwin Osgood Grover*, 135
Do You Fear the Wind? .... *Hamlin Garland*, 109
Dreams of the Sea .... *William H. Davies*, 76

Early Morning at Bargis .... *Hermann Hagedorn*, 143
Early Spring .... *Alfred Tennyson*, 205
Ellis Park .... *Helen Hoyt*, 132
Epitaph, The .... *Katherine Tynan*, 267
Evening in Tyringham Valley .... *Richard Watson Gilder*, 231

Farewell .... *Katherine Tynan*, 96
Farewell .... *Harry Kemp*, 251
Far in a Western Brookland .... *A. E. Housman*, 274

Far from the Madding Crowd .... *Nixon Waterman,* 148
Faun, The .... *Richard Hovey,* 12
Fiddling Lad, The .... *Adelaide Crapsey,* 153
Fishing .... *Edgar A. Guest,* 169
Fishing .... *Edgar A. Guest,* 16
Flood Tide .... *Marjorie Alice Miller,* 105
Flower Chorus .... *Ralph Waldo Emerson,* 191
Folly .... *Vivian Yeiser Laramore,* 243
Full Heart, The .... *Robert Nichols,* 256

Gipsy Feet .... *Fannie Stearns Davis,* 158
Gipsy-Heart .... *Katharine Lee Bates,* 172
Gipsying, The .... *Theodosia Garrison,* 175
Gipsy Song .... *Sara Hamilton Birchall,* 156
Gipsy Trail, The .... *Rudyard Kipling,* 166
Gipsy Wedding, The .... *Sara Hamilton Birchall,* 165
Girl in a Tree .... *Frances Frost,* 59
God is at the Anvil .... *Lew Sarett,* 253
God Made This Day for me ....*Edgar A. Guest,* 34
God, When You Thought of a Pine Tree .... *Unknown,* 63
God's World .... *Edna St. Vincent Millay,* 249
Going Down in Ships .... *Harry Kemp,* 77
Going of His Feet, The .... *Harry Kemp,* 134
Good-Bye .... *Ralph Waldo Emerson,* 270
Good Company .... *Karl Wilson Baker,* 71
Gospel of the Fields .... *Arthur Upson,* 247
Grace for Gardens .... *Louise Driscoll,* 40
Grass, The .... *Walt Whitman,* 47
"Gratias Ago" .... *Geoffrey Howard,* 260
Gray .... *Oscar Williams,* 85
Gray Rocks and Grayer Sea .... *Charles G. D. Roberts,* 89
Great Outdoors, The .... *Maud Russell,* 29
Green Inn, The .... *Theodosia Garrison,* 18
Green Tree in the Fall, The .... *Jessie B. Rittenhouse,* 72

Had I the Choice .... *Walt Whitman,* 84
Happy Wind .... *William H. Davies,* 112
Hark! Hark! .... *Leonora Speyer,* 273
Hark to the Shouting Wind .... *Henry Timrod,* 109
Have You? .... *Harry W. Dean,* 171
Hesperides .... *Harry Kemp,* 257
Highways .... *Leslie Nelson Jennings,* 8

Hills ....Arthur Guiterman, 121
Hills, The ....Theodosia Garrison, 125
Hill Hunger ....Joseph Auslander, 124
Hollyhocks, The ....Ray Laurence, 48
Homesick ....Julia C. R. Dorr, 258
Hound, The ....Babette Deutsch, 229
House of the Trees, The ....Ethelwyn Wetherald, 64
How Miracles Abound ....Clinton Scollard, 236
Hunting Song ....Richard Hovey, 31

I Am Weary of Being Bitter ....Arthur Davison Ficke, 275
If all the Skies ....Henry van Dyke, 259
I Meant to do My Work Today ....Richard LeGallienne, 111
Immortal, The ....Cale Young Rice, 196
I Must Out and Play Again ....Kathleen Millay, 2
In a Garden ....Theda Kenyon, 50
In City Streets ....Ada Smith, 20
Indian Summer ....Emily Dickinson, 225
In Spring-Time ....W. H. Davies, 1

Journey ....Edna St. Vincent Millay, 145
Joys of the Road, The ....Bliss Carman, 136

King's Highway, The ....John Steven McGroarty, 32

Lake, The ....Eleanour Norton, 29
Lark, The ....Lizette Woodworth Reese, 250
Last Hour, The ....Ethel Clifford, 252
Let me Go Where'er I Will ....Ralph Waldo Emerson, 233
Lilac, The ....Humbert Wolfe, 48
Little Things ....Orrick Johns, 236

Maine Trail, A ....Gertrude H. McGiffert, 27
Mangroves Dance, The ....Rose Strong Hubbell, 37
Marigolds ....Bliss Carman, 49
Marshes, The ....Sidney Lanier, 238
May-Lure ....Richard Burton, 211
Memory ....Siegfried Sassoon, 272
Mendicants, The ....Bliss Carman, 176
More Ancient Mariner, A ....Bliss Carman, 173
Morning, A ....Theodosia Garrison, 114
Morning Song ....Lancaster Pollard, 186

Most-Sacred Mountain, The ....*Eunice Tietjens,* 127
Mountain Sat, The ....*Emily Dickinson,* 118
My Garden ....*Thomas E. Brown,* 41
My Heart Leaps Up When I Behold ....*William Wordsworth,* 238
Mystic, The ....*Cale Young Rice,* 115

Naturalist on a June Sunday, The ....*Leonora Speyer,* 215
Noise of Leaves, The ....*George Dillon,* 273
November in England ....*Thomas Hood,* 228

Ocean, The ....*Lord Byron,* 100
O Dreamy, Gloomy, Friendly Trees ....*Herbert Trench,* 62
Old Age ....*Cale Young Rice,* 182
On a Hill ....*Irene Rutherford McLeod,* 126
One Blackbird ....*Harold Monro,* 243
One Kind of Humility ....*Jean Starr Untermeyer,* 118
Out in the Fields with God ....*Louise Imogen Guiney,* 53
Out-of-doors ....*Ethel E. Mannin,* 239
Overtones ....*William Alexander Percy,* 218

Pagan Hymn, A ....*John Runcie,* 85
Path that Leads to Nowhere, The ....*Corinne Roosevelt Robinson,* 9
Perilous Light, The ....*Eva Gore-Booth,* 241
Picture, The ....*Frederick O. Sylvester,* 245
Pippa's Song ....*Robert Browning,* 233
Pool, The ....*Marjorie Pickthall,* 179
Port o' Hearts Desire, The ....*John Steven McGroarty,* 99
Prairie Sunset, A ....*E. J. Pratt,* 232
Prayer, A ....*Edwin Markham,* 57
Prayer Before Poems ....*Anne Blackwell Payne,* 235

Ragged Regiment, The ....*Alice Williams Brotherton,* 49
Rain ....*Kenneth Slade Alling,* 250
Rain ....*Lucy Larcom,* 44
Rebellion ....*Stephen Chalmers,* 140
Renewal ....*Charles Hanson Towne,* 195
Return, The ....*Algernon Charles Swinburne,* 97
Reveille ....*Louis Untermeyer,* 36
Rhodora ....*Ralph Waldo Emerson,* 52
Road Song ....*James Stuart Montgomery,* 22
Road Song ....*W. G. Tinckom-Fernandez,* 24
Road that Leads to Home, The ....*Ethel E. Mannin,* 150

Road to Vagabondia, The	*Dana Burnet*, 157
Roaring Frost, The	*Alice Meynell*, 107
Robin, The	*Emily Dickinson*, 54
Runaway, The	*Cale Young Rice*, 188
Rune of Riches, A	*Florence Converse*, 244
Sea Call	*Margaret Widdemer*, 79
Sea Change	*Dorothy Peace*, 103
Sea, The	*Bryan Waller Proctor*, 89
Sea, The	*Richard Hovey*, 92
Sea, The	*Nora Hopper*, 81
Sea-Chill	*Arthur Guiterman*, 129
Sea-Fever	*John Masefield*, 75
Sea Longing	*Harold Vinal*, 84
Sea Road, The	*Martha Haskell Clark*, 91
Sea-Song	*Martha Haskell Clark*, 104
Sea-Urge	*Unknown*, 100
Sea Wind, The	*Arthur Ketchum*, 111
Secret, The	*John Richard Moreland*, 193
Secret Voices, The	*Ethel E. Mannin*, 178
September	*Sara Hamilton Birchall*, 223
Shared	*Lucy Larcom*, 265
Shepherds Who Pastures Seek	*Herbert Trench*, 268
Ship-Love	*Ethel E. Mannin*, 80
Short Beach	*Richard Hovey*, 79
"Sic Vita"	*William Stanley Braithwaite*, 245
Singer's Quest, The	*Odell Shepard*, 3
Sojourner, The	*Sara Hamilton Birchall*, 146
Song	*Georgiana Goddard King*, 19
Song	*John Vance Cheney*, 239
Song in Autumn, A	*Theodosia Garrison*, 219
Song in March	*Clinton Scollard*, 190
Song of Ballyshannon	*Jeanne Robert Foster*, 261
Song of Desire, A	*Frederic Lawrence Knowles*, 102
Song of Early Autumn, A	*Richard Watson Gilder*, 181
Song of the Open	*Sara Hamilton Birchall*, 139
Song of the Open Road, A	*Louis J. McQuilland*, 25
Song of the Open Road	*Ogden Nash*, 153
Song of the Road, A	*Fred G. Bowles*, 263
Song of the Sea	*Richard Burton*, 95
Song the Grass Sings, A	*Charles G. Blanden*, 42
Son of the Sea, A	*Bliss Carman*, 75

Sorrow in a Garden	*May Riley Smith*, 213
South Wind	*Siegfried Sassoon*, 107
Spell of the Pool, The	*L. Burton Crane, Jr.* 28
Spring	*Norman Gale*, 193
Spring	*Richard Hovey*, 196
Spring	*Henry Timrod*, 206
Spring's Answer	*Edwin Osgood Grover*, 185
Spring Market	*Louise Driscoll*, 189
Spring Song	*Bliss Carman*, 200
St. Bartholomew's on the Hill	*Bliss Carman*, 168
Streams	*Clinton Scollard*, 149
Strip of Blue, A	*Lucy Larcom*, 160
Summer	*Richard Burton*, 216
Sunflowers	*Clinton Scollard*, 43
Sunrise	*Edgar A. Guest*, 234
Sunrise	*Robert Browning*, 212
Sweet, Low Speech of the Rain, The	*Ella Higginson*, 203

Tell all the World	*Harry Kemp*, 213
Thanks	*Norman Gale*, 276
That Time of Year	*William Shakespeare*, 256
That Wind is Best	*Caroline Atherton Mason*, 112
Three Trees	*Christopher Morley*, 68
Throstle, The	*Alfred Tennyson*, 212
Time and Spirit	*Léonie Adams*, 256
Toil of the Trail	*Hamlin Garland*, 4
Traveller's Joy	*Arthur Ketchum*, 131
Traveller's Rest	*C. Fox-Smith*, 147
Trees	*Bliss Carman*, 65
Trees, The	*Lucy Larcom*, 71
Trees, The	*Samuel Valentine Cole*, 67
Trees	*Henry van Dyke*, 70
Trees and the Master, The	*Sidney Lanier*, 66
Tree-Feelings	*Charlotte Perkins Gilman*, 61
Tree-Top Road	*May Riley Smith*, 142
Trumpet of the Dawn	*Clinton Scollard*, 265
Turn o' the Year, The	*Katherine Tynan*, 183
Twilight of the Wood	*Léonie Adams*, 60
Twilight Sea	*Amelia C. Welby*, 103
Two Old Men	*Louise Driscoll*, 5

Undersong, The	*Fiona MacLeod*, 88
Up-Hill	*Christina Rossetti*, 266

Up a Hill and a Hill ....*Fannie Stearns Davis*, 120
Up, Up! My Friend and Quit Your Books .*William Wordsworth*, 21

Vagabond at Home, The ....*Ruth Wright Kauffman*, 165
Vagabond, The ....*Edgar A. Guest*, 155
Vagabonds ....*Sara Hamilton Birchall*, 175
Vagabond Song, A ....*Bliss Carman*, 171
Vagrant, The ....*Pauline Slender*, 164

Walking at Night ....*Amory Hare*, 23
Wanderer, The ....*Zoe Akins*, 264
Wander-Lure, The ....*Kendall Banning*, 162
Wanderlust ....*Isabel Ecclestine Mackay*, 19
Wanderer's Song, A ....*John Masefield*, 3
Wander-thirst ....*Gerald Gould*, 155
Wasted Hours ....*Medora Addison*, 253
Waves of Breffny, The ....*Eva Gore-Booth*, 78
Welcome, The ....*Arthur Powell*, 248
Wet Sheet and a Flowing Sea, A ....*Allan Cunningham*, 87
What do We Plant ....*Henry Abbey*, 69
Where Lies the Land? ....*Arthur Hugh Clough*, 151
Whisper of Earth, The ....*Edward J. O'Brien*, 234
White Armour ....*Jean Starr Untermeyer*, 268
Who Hath Seen the Wind? ....*Christina Rossetti*, 110
Whole Duty of Berkshire Brooks, The .*Grace Hazard Conkling*, 240
Who Plants a Dogwood Tree ....*Mabel Brown*, 38
Wind ....*John Galsworthy*, 110
Wind-Litany ....*Margaret Widdemer*, 113
Wind's Life, The ....*Harry Kemp*, 115
Wishing ....*William Allingham*, 44
World is Too Much With Us, The ....*William Wordsworth*, 94
Word with a Skylark, A ....*Sarah Piatt*, 241

Year In, Year Out ....*Kathleen Millay*, 60
Year's Awakening, The ....*Thomas Hardy*, 184
Yellow Pansy, A ....*Helen Gray Cone*, 56
Yellow Warblers ....*Katharine Lee Bates*, 36
Young Dandelions, The ....*Dina Muloch Craik*, 42
Young Sea ....*Carl Sandburg*, 74

Index by First Lines

A bleak wind is riding on the waves, 85
Above the crestward-climbing pines, 265
Above the shouting of the gale, 73
A child said *What is the grass?* fetching it to me with full hands, 47
A close gray sky, 250
A day to dream, 16
A flock of winds came winging from the North, 107
Afoot and light-hearted, I take to the open road, 9
Again among the hills!, 122
A Garden is a lovesome thing, Got wot!, 41
A little road goes up the hill, 55
Alive in space against his will, 273
All the golden weather, forth let us ride to-day, 32
All the lanes are lyric, 193
Alone on the shore in the pause of the nighttime, 256
An altered look about the hills, 210
April, April, 208
April comes with sudden showers, 192
April, when I heard, 195
Autumn, Autumn, give me of your crimson, 219
Autumn, in her scarlet cloak, 219
A wet sheet and a flowing sea,—, 87
A Wind's in the heart of me, a fire's in my heels, 3

Bartholomew, my brother, 168
Beyond the blue rim of the world, 257
Beyond the East the sunrise, beyond the West the sea, 155
Bring me the sunset in a cup, 130
By sea and by land, 216

Clear air and grassy lea, 143
Come follow, heart upon your sleeve, 27
Come, let's get out of here, Out of the din of it, 10
Come, spur away, 30
Comes the lure of green things growing, 39
Come with me, follow me, swift as a moth, 179

Day!, 94
Day!, 212
Dear common flower, that grow'st beside the way, 45
Death is like moonlight in a lofty wood, 275
Demand no bay or laurel now, 268
Did you forget to bud in Spring, 72
Does the road wind-up all the way?, 266
Down around the quay they lie, the ships that sail to sea, 99
Down east and up along the fringy coast of Maine, 135
Do you fear the force of the wind, 109

Far in a western brookland, 274

Gipsy, gipsy, gipsy girl!, 156
Give me the clear blue sky overhead, and the long road to my feet, 24
God is at the anvil, beating out the sun;, 253
God spreads a carpet soft and green, 248
God, when you thought of a pine tree, 63
Going down to sea in ships, 77
Good-bye, proud world! I'm going home:, 270
Gray rocks, and grayer sea, 89
Great Author of a world, of sky, of sea;, 235

Had I the choice to tally greatest bards, 84
Hark to the shouting Wind!, 109
Has your dinner lost its savor?, 17
Have you ever built a camp-fire at the closing of the day?, 171
Have you ever thought, my friend, 247
Have you gazed on naked grandeur where there's nothing else to gaze on, 13
Have you heard the secret voices go whispering in your blood, 178
Have you heard the calling, calling, of the Distance, 31
Heart free, hand free, 245
Heaven is in my hand, and I, 246
Heavy with unshed tears—weary with pain, 103
Here in the country's heart, 35
Here to this ancient garden, 213
Her legs were long, 59

He was sitting on a doorstep as I went strolling by;, 157
His feet went here and there, 134
How do you know that the pilgrim track, 184
How miracles abound, 236
How the heart pulls at its tether, 211

I am a bold fellow, 42
I am homesick for the mountains—, 119
I am tired of planning and toiling, 7
I am wearied with insatiable longing, 82
I am weary of being bitter and weary of being wise, 275
I believe, 247
I call thee from the changing land, 81
I do not own an inch of land, 150
If all the skies were sunshine, 259
If this be all, for which I've listened long, 241
I have a golden ball, 245
I have an understanding with the hills, 263
I have drunk the Sea's good wine, 85
I have heard the wild geese, 182
I have ridden the wind, 115
I heard a bird at break of day, 218
I heard God calling, 185
I hear the sea-song of the blood in my heart, 88
I know not why I yearn for thee again, 76
I lift my cap to Beauty, 263

I like a road thet leads away to prospects white and fair, 6
I like the tangled brakes and briers, 224
I love the ragged veterans of June, 49
I love the silver-shaken, 115
I love the stony pasture, 226
I meant to do my work to-day—, 111
I must down to the seas again, to the lonely sea and the sky, 75
I must get out to the woods again, to the whispering tree and the birds awing, 150
I must go down to the seas again, where the billows romp and reel, 129
I must out and play again into the salt sea air!, 2
I never knew how words were vain, 250
I never loved your plains!—, 121
Interminable, not to be divined, 92
In the far corner, 54
In the Garden of Eden, planted by God, 65
In the misty hollow, shyly greening branches, 234
In this world I shall not find, 113
Into the woods my Master went, 66
I said in my heart, "I am sick of four walls and a ceiling., 196
I said it in the meadow-path, 265
Is it raining, little flower?—, 44
I sing the first green leaf upon the bough, 190
I so love water-laughter, 149
I think that I shall never see, 153

It is not down this road I walk, 144
It is not raining rain for me, 209
It is pleasant to lie in the gloaming, 203
It's foolish to bring money, 189
It's home for me and a snug roof-tree, 22
It seems to me I'd like to go, 148
I've been wandering, listening for a song, 3
I want to stride the hills! My feet cry out, 124
I was born for deep-sea faring;, 75
I will be the gladdest thing, 125
I will go back to the great sweet mother, 97
I will go out to grass with that old King, 12
I will leave the dust of the city street and the noise of the busy town, 164
I wish we might go gypsying one day while we're young—, 175
I wonder if they like it—being trees?, 61
I would spend a morning, 210

Jes' the sort o' weather and jes' the sort o' sky, 34

Lavender for old loves, 57
Leaf is no more now than corruption's scent, 60
Let me go where'er I will, 233
Life's sweetest joys are hidden, 142
Little masters, hat in hand, 55
Little park that I pass through, 132

Long is the road 'twixt town and town that runs, 133
Lord God in Paradise, 40

Make me over, mother April, 200
Many a tree is found in the wood, 70
Men travel far and far away, 5
"Men will grow weary," said the Lord, 169
Midnight—the black, dead vast of night, 227
My face is wet with the rain, 23
My heart leaps up when I behold, 238
My old gardener leans on his hoe, 215
My old love for the water has come back again—, 79
My road is a by-road, with big trees reading high, 150
My shoes fall on the house-top that is so far beneath me, 117
My tall sunflowers love the sun, 43
My tent stands in a garden, 220

No sight of it, only the song, 273
No sun—no moon!, 228
Not soon shall I forget—a sheet, 96
Now the joys of the road are chiefly these:, 136

O dreamy, gloomy, friendly trees, 62
O give me the Pole Star overhead, 82
O Great outdoors without floors, 29
Oh, gipsy hearts are many enough, but gipsy feet are few!, 158
Oh, green curved the hill road and beckoned to my feet, 91
Oh, happy wind, how sweet, 112
Oh, hush, my heart, and take thine ease, 194
Oh, it's spring once more in France, and it's spring in gay Algiers, 165
Oh, the salt wind in my nostrils!, 79
Oh, to feel the tremble of a ship beneath my feet again, 100
Oh, who will lodge at my Inn tonight, 146
Oh would you stay indoor, indoor, 31
O joys of love and joys of fame, 253
O my garden! lying whitely in the moonlight and the dew, 258
O my Soul, let us go unto our hills, 125
Once more the gipsy aster, 165
Once more the Heavenly Power, 205
One time when I was sick, 237
On that first day so singular, 193
Ope your doors and take me in, 64
O such a commotion under the ground, 191
Outside here in the city the burning pavements lie, 15
Over the shoulders and slopes of the dune, 53
O world, I cannot hold thee close enough!, 249

Rhodora! is the sages ask thee why, 52

Ring-ting! I wish I were a primrose, 44

Shall we say heaven is not heaven, 118
Shepherds who pastures seek, 268
She was born inland in the open country., 105
Since of earth, air and water, 260
Sky!, 50
Some are sick for Spring and warm winds blowing, 229
Something calls and whispers, along the city street, 19
Something tapped at my window pane, 195
Sometime we shall remember them, the little camping places, 161
Soon, ah, soon the April weather, 186
Space, and the twelve clean winds of heaven, 127
Spindle-wood, spindle-wood, will you lend me, pray, 228
Spirit going with me here, 255
Spring has come up from the South again, 196
Spring on a wind-swept hill!, 126
Spring, with that nameless pathos in the air, 206
"Summer is coming, summer is coming, 212

Take me home to Ballyshannon, for there's music in the word;, 261
Teach me, Father, how to go, 57
Tell all the world that summer's here again, 213
Tell them, O Sky-born, when I die, 251
Thank you very much indeed, 276
That time of year thou mayst in me behold, 256
The April world is misted with emerald and gold;, 172
The birds of the air, they sing it, 239
The charm is working, now, 41
The day is done, and the darkness, 271
The Eternal Beauty smiled on me, 241
The first faint dawn was flushing up the skies, 35
The glad, mad wind went singing by, 114
The grand road from the mountain goes shining to the sea, 78
The grass is taller, greener, 186
The highways and the byways, the kind sky folding all, 19
The hollyhocks are standing, 48
The lights are on the harbor, 105
The little cares that fretted me, 53
The long-winged terns dart wild and dire, 86
The lyric sound of laughter, 183
The mangroves dance in the light of the moon, 37
The marigolds are nodding:, 49
The moon has made me weary, 243
The morns are meeker than they were, 218
The mountain sat upon the plain, 118
The northeast wind was the wind off the lake, 108

The old Earth-Mother calls us, 25
The poplar is a French tree, 68
There is a lake—but I forgot its name, 29
There is a pleasure in the pathless woods, 100
There is something in the autumn that is native to my blood—, 171
There'll be no roof to shelter you;, 153
There must be fairy miners, 47
There's a crystal-arrowed riffle at the turning of the river, 28
There's a path that leads to nowhere, 9
"There's a pool in the ancient forest," 245
There's a whisper in the orchard, there's a laughter in the breeze, 139
There's many a pool that holds a cloud, 1
There's nothing very beautiful and nothing very gay, 236
There's something in a noble tree—, 67
There was a day I wasted long ago, 253
The robin is the one, 54
The robin's on the wing again; I hear the call o' spring again, 162
The roof is high and arched and blue, 18
The sea is never still, 74
These are the days when birds come back, 225
The Sea! the Sea! the open Sea!, 89
The ships are lying in the bay, 264
The song of the sea was an ancient song, 95
The Spring blew trumpets of color;, 199
The stars must make an awful noise, 243
The swarthy bee is a buccaneer, 173
The trees are God's great alphabet:, 62
The violet is much too shy, 42
The twilight hours, like birds, flew by, 103
The white moth to the closing vine, 166
The World is too much with us; late and soon, 94
The wind comes up across the hill, the wind goes laughing by., 223
They cannot change the hills; though they may hew, 257
The year's at the spring, 233
This is the time when bit by bit, 183
Thou dreamer with the million moods, 102
Time is never wasted listening to the trees;, 71
To build the trout a crystal stair;, 240
To-day I have grown taller from walking with the trees, 71
Today I saw the sun come up, like Neptune from the sea., 234
To-day was a sea-gull day, dear heart, to-day was a sea-gull day, 104
To the wall of the old green garden, 56

To tread the path of glory needs a braver soul than I, 155
To wake at morn, 140

Until the day the world shall die, 163
Up a hill and a hill there's a sudden orchard-slope, 120
Upon a showery night and still, 51
Upon us vagabonds who take, 175
Up! Up! my friend, and quit your books, 21

We are as mendicants who wait, 176
We see them not—we cannot hear, 249
What alchemist could in one hour so drain, 232
What are you doing, little day-moon, 188
What came ye out for to seek, O Maker of Words?, 239
What domes and pinnacles of mist and fire, 231
What do we plant when we plant the tree?, 69
What have I gained by the toil of the trail?, 4
What sudden bugle calls us in the night, 36
What went you, Pilgrim, for to see?, 131
When God gave to all men, 80

When I am overmatched by petty cares, 251
When I was young my heart and head were light, 272
When late in summer the streams run yellow, 181
When you are tired of the long road and the open sky, 147
Where have you been, South Wind, this May-day morning?, 107
Where lies the land to which the ship would go?, 151
Whichever way the wind doth blow, 112
Who has seen the wind?, 110
Who plants a dogwood tree holds hands with God, 38
Who's learned the lure of trodden ways, 8
Who thought of the lilac?, 48
Wind, wind—heather gipsy, 110
Winnow me through with thy keen clear breath, 111
Write on my grave when I am dead, 267

Year in, year out, 60
Ye marshes, how candid and simple and nothing-withholding and free, 238
Yonder in the heather there's a bed for sleeping, 20
You who are inland born know not the pain, 84
You who were once so careless, I can recall you now, 177

Southeastern Community
College Library
Whiteville, NC 28472